GREAT TASTES

CHICKEN

First published in 2009 by Bay Books, an imprint of Murdoch Books Pty Limited
This edition published in 2010.

Murdoch Books Australia
Pier 8/9
23 Hickson Road
Millers Point NSW 2000
Phone: +61 (0) 2 8220 2000
Fax: +61 (0) 2 8220 2558
www.murdochbooks.com.au

Murdoch Books UK Limited
Erico House, 6th Floor
93–99 Upper Richmond Road
Putney, London SW15 2TG
Phone: +44 (0) 20 8785 5995
Fax: +44 (0) 20 8785 5985
www.murdochbooks.co.uk

Chief Executive: Juliet Rogers
Publishing Director: Kay Scarlett
Publisher: Lynn Lewis
Senior Designer: Heather Menzies
Designer: Wendy Inkster
Production: Kita George

ISBN: 9780681657748

PRINTED IN CHINA

IMPORTANT: Those who might be at risk from the effects of salmonella poisoning (the elderly, pregnant women, young children and those suffering from immune deficiency diseases) should consult their doctor with any concerns about eating raw eggs.

OVEN GUIDE: You may find cooking times vary depending on the oven you are using. For fan-forced ovens, as a general rule, set the oven temperature to 20°C (35°F) lower than indicated in the recipe.

GREAT TASTES

CHICKEN

More than 120 easy recipes for every day

bay books

CONTENTS

CHICKEN BASICS

Chicken is a versatile food which lends itself to many types of recipes, methods of cooking and styles of cuisine from around the world. This comprehensive guide to cooking with chicken includes information on the different types of cuts available and on purchasing, storing and cooking chicken. It will help you to prepare successful and delicious dishes every time.

Here is advice on how to get the best out of chicken: what to look for when buying and how to store and prepare your purchase prior to cooking. There's also information on how to make stock and gravy, jointing and boning chickens, and the art of carving.

Purchasing

There is a wide variety of chickens and chicken cuts available.

Young tender birds are good for grilling, barbecuing, frying and roasting. Chickens over 1.8 kg (3 lb 10 oz) are usually only suitable for poaching, braising or boiling because of their tough flesh (although they have excellent flavour) and are labelled as boiling fowls. Unless you specifically want a very large bird, buy two smaller chickens rather than one large one.

Whole baby chickens (or poussins) weigh about 500 g (1 lb) and serve one person. Chickens under 1.5 kg (3 lb) serve two to four people. Whole roasting chickens weighing over 1.5 kg (3 lb) should serve at least four people.

Chickens are sold cleaned, with their innards removed. The neck is usually tucked inside. Sometimes the giblets are in the cavity, contained in a plastic bag, so be sure to remove them before cooking or freezing.

Whole birds are marketed by weight, and the weight becomes the number of the chicken. For example, a No. 10 chicken weighs 1 kg (2 lb); a No. 16 chicken weighs 1.6 kg (3¼ lb), and so on.

When buying chicken by weight, check whether the giblets are with the bird. Giblets weigh approximately 175 g (6 oz) and will affect the number of portions you get after cooking.

Fresh chicken

Fresh chicken has better flavour and texture than frozen. Look for skin that is light pink and moist, rather than wet, with no dry spots. It should be unbroken and free from blemishes and bruises. The breast should be plump and well rounded; on a young bird, the point of the breastbone will be flexible.

At speciality poultry shops you can buy free-range, grain-fed, and corn-fed chickens (with yellow skin and flesh).

Chicken can also be purchased cooked. Hot take-away barbecued, roasted or chargrilled chicken has become a mainstay as the basis for quick meals. Cooked, smoked chicken is available whole, chilled, from delicatessens and supermarkets.

Chicken cuts include: double or single breasts on the bone, with skin or without; breast fillets; tenderloins (the part just behind the breast); marylands (the whole thigh and leg); thigh cutlets; thigh fillets; wings; and drumsticks (the bottom part of the leg). Buy the appropriate cut of chicken for the cooking process you will be using. It is not always necessary to buy the most expensive fillets to produce an excellent result. Here is a guide to the cuts used in this book:

FOR ROASTING – whole roasting chickens, baby chickens, whole breasts, wings, marylands, drumsticks, thighs.

FOR GRILLING – chicken halves and quarters, wings, drumsticks, marylands, thigh cutlets.

FOR BARBECUING – chicken halves, whole breasts, wings, drumsticks, marylands, thigh cutlets, tenderloins.

FOR STIR-FRYING – breast fillets, thigh fillets, tenderloins, livers.

FOR PAN-FRYING – marylands, breast fillets, tenderloins, livers.

FOR DEEP-FRYING – drumsticks, wings, thighs, chicken pieces.

FOR CASSEROLES/BRAISING – whole chickens, chicken pieces, thighs, thigh cutlets, drumsticks, wings.

FOR POACHING – whole chickens, whole breasts, breast fillets, thighs, drumsticks.

FOR STOCK – bones, necks, giblets, boiling fowls.

The three basic chicken sizes, from left to right: large boiling fowl; roasting chicken; baby chicken or poussin.

Chicken leg cuts, clockwise from left: thigh (underside view), drumstick, leg quarter (maryland), thigh fillet, thigh.

Storing fresh chicken

Chicken must be transported home as quickly as possible. Do not leave it sitting in the sun in the car or car boot. The internal temperature of a car left closed in full sun spells disaster to all chicken products. The longer that food spends between 5°C (41°F) and 60°C (140°F), the greater the likelihood of rapid growth of harmful bacteria that may result in food poisoning.

Keep chicken away from any strong-smelling items such as cleaning agents and petrol that you may have stored in your vehicle; chicken will absorb the smells.

Make it your policy to purchase chicken or meat as the last item on your round of shopping. In hot weather, use an insulated chiller bag to keep it cold.

It is particularly important to store poultry carefully to avoid contamination by salmonella bacteria, which can cause food poisoning. Always wash hands, chopping boards, knives and cooking implements in very hot soapy water after handling raw chicken. Always keep cooked and raw chicken separate.

Before storing uncooked whole chicken, discard the tight plastic wrappings and pour off any juices. Remove the neck and giblets from whole birds (sometimes these are in a plastic bag inside the cavity). Giblets should be cooked immediately or stored separately. Use the neck and giblets for stock; chop the liver to flavour a sauce, gravy or stuffing.

Loosely wrap the chicken in plastic wrap or place in a plastic bag, place the package on a plate and refrigerate on the bottom shelf of the refrigerator. Never place uncooked chicken where the juices could drip on or otherwise come into contact with other foodstuffs. A fresh, cleaned and wrapped chicken can be stored in the refrigerator for up to two days.

To store fresh chicken pieces or cuts, remove them from trays or any other packaging, pour off any juices and loosely wrap in plastic wrap or place in a plastic bag. Refrigerate for up to two days.

Storing cooked chicken

Chicken should stand no more than an hour at room temperature after cooking. If keeping longer than this, store it loosely wrapped in the refrigerator and use within three days. The chicken does not have to be cold when it goes into the refrigerator. If the chicken has a sauce or stuffing, it should be eaten within 24 hours of cooking. Stuffing and gravy should be stored separately.

Frozen chicken

Make sure that any frozen chicken you buy from the supermarket freezer is solid and completely enclosed in its packaging. Do not purchase any that appear semi-soft and that are sitting in their own juices, as this indicates that they have been in the display cabinet for longer than is ideal.

Uncooked, home-frozen chicken (without giblets) will keep for up to nine months in good condition. Remove the giblets before freezing as they will begin to deteriorate after eight weeks.

If a package has partly defrosted it must never be refrozen; defrost fully in the refrigerator and cook promptly. Stuffed birds should never be frozen, as the filling will not freeze enough to prevent the development of harmful bacteria.

Freezing fresh chicken: Have the freezer temperature at minus 15°C (5°F) or lower. Use heavy-gauge polythene bags and good-quality plastic wrap to package fresh chicken.

Label each package with the details of the contents, the date it was packaged and stored and either the number of people it will feed or the unfrozen weight. Use a waterproof pen or wax crayon.

It is important to expel as much air as possible from the packaging; oxygen left behind will speed up the process of oxidisation of any fat, resulting in an unpleasant taste after prolonged storing. If you do a lot of freezing, it may be worthwhile investing in a vacuum freezer pump to efficiently expel air.

Secure freezer bags by twisting the tips and closing them with masking tape; this is preferable to metal twist ties. Or, clip a metal band in place with a clipping device.

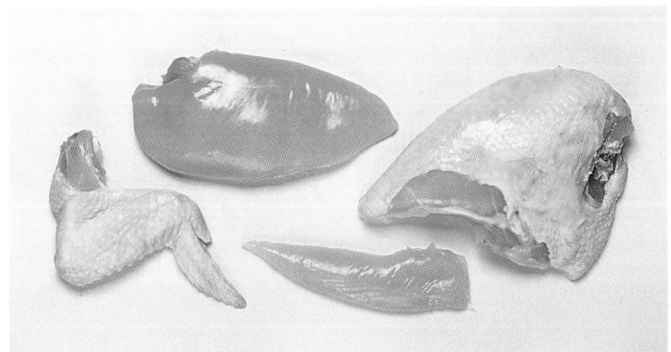

Chicken breast and wing cuts, clockwise from left: wing, single breast fillet, whole breast bone, tenderloin.

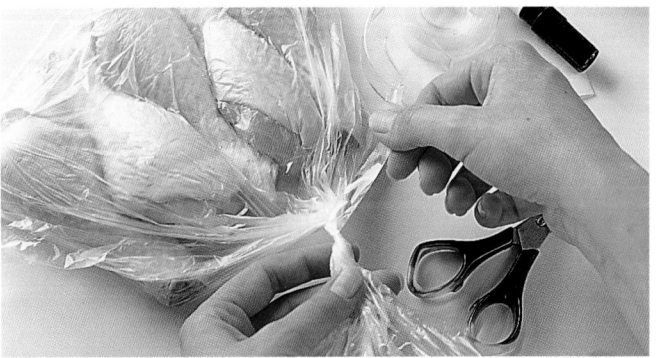

To freeze uncooked chicken, wrap in heavy-duty plastic bags. Remove the giblets as they begin to deteriorate after eight weeks.

Wrap the chicken in heavy-gauge freezer bags or good-quality plastic wrap, then in aluminium foil, expelling air. Label and freeze. Remove the giblets and neck and pack separately to be used for stock.

Commercially frozen whole chickens without giblets can be kept for nine months, or according to instructions on the package. If the chicken is still frozen hard, place it in the freezer in its original wrappings as soon as possible after purchase. If it has started to thaw, place it in the refrigerator to completely thaw out, cook it promptly, cool quickly, wrap and refreeze it. Never refreeze thawed, uncooked poultry.

Whole chickens can be trussed before freezing to be ready for cooking when thawed. To provide convenient serving portions and to save space, cut the chicken into four, eight or 10 pieces before freezing. Wrap each joint individually in plastic wrap, expelling air, and then combine in a larger package in a sturdy plastic bag. Seal, tape the end of the bag to the package, label and freeze.

Chicken cuts such as legs or wings can be frozen either as individual portions or in amounts to serve several people. Wrap portions individually in plastic wrap, expelling air, then place them in a larger plastic bag. Seal and tape the end of the bag to the package. Label and freeze.

Boneless cuts can be cut into strips or cubes before freezing. Weigh out meal-sized portions and place in heavy-duty plastic bags. Fill right to the corners with chicken. Flatten the package (so it will defrost quickly) and expel the air. Seal, label and freeze. The same procedure applies to chicken mince.

Freezing cooked chicken

Cooked whole chickens or chicken pieces can be frozen with or without bones, for up to two weeks. After this time, the flesh will tend to dry out.

Moist chicken dishes such as stews, casseroles, curries and soups are all suitable for freezing. Quickly reduce the temperature of the cooked item by placing it in the refrigerator or by plunging the base of the dish into cold water, then cool completely in the refrigerator. Line cake tins or other suitable

containers with a heavy-duty plastic bag. Spoon portions into the bag and expel the air. Seal, label and freeze. Place the bag in its tin into the freezer. When completely frozen, remove from the tin, reseal to remove as much air as possible and return, labelled, to the freezer.

Or, simply spoon the meat directly into plastic or aluminium containers and seal, label and freeze. As a general rule, freeze cooked chicken for a maximum of two months.

Defrosting

Frozen chicken must be completely thawed in the refrigerator before cooking; allow two to three hours per 500 g (1 lb). A frozen chicken should be cooked within 12 hours of thawing. Do not thaw chicken at room temperature. Never keep perishable food at room temperature for longer than two hours, particularly on hot days. This includes time to prepare, serve and eat.

Microwave defrosting is not recommended for whole frozen chickens because of uneven thawing. However, smaller packages of cuts or pre-cooked meals can be successfully thawed in the microwave using the defrost setting. Always remove chicken from wrapping before defrosting. Stir casseroles occasionally to distribute heat evenly. Separate joints or pieces as they soften.

Preparation

Before cooking a chicken, remove the neck, giblets and fat pockets from the cavity. Discard the fat and use the neck and giblets for stock. Remove any excess fat and sinew from chicken pieces.

Raw poultry should be wiped with a damp cloth, rather than washed, before cooking. Wipe frozen chickens with paper towels to absorb excess moisture.

Use a cook's knife for jointing uncooked chickens. Poultry shears are excellent for dividing whole chickens into serving portions, especially for splitting the breastbone, cutting the backbone and rib bones and cutting the breast and legs in half.

Stuffing a whole chicken before roasting adds extra flavour and plumps up the chicken. Do not stuff a chicken more than three hours before cooking. If using warm stuffing, the chicken

To freeze cooked dishes, place them into airtight plastic or aluminium containers.

To marinate, pour the liquid over the chicken in a non-metallic dish, such as one made of glass or ceramic.

must be cooked immediately. Stuffed, or stuffed and trussed chickens take a little longer to cook than unstuffed chickens. The juices from the cavity of the chicken will soak into the stuffing, so the stuffing must be cooked through to prevent contamination by harmful salmonella bacteria.

Some people prefer chicken without the skin. Removing the skin eliminates much of the fat from the chicken, as the fat lies in a layer just underneath the skin. Usually the skin is removed after cooking, but drumsticks can be skinned and then cooked.

To remove the skin from drumsticks, use a small sharp knife. Begin by carefully loosening the skin from the flesh at the large joint end. Then pull the skin down and away from the flesh. Some specialty chicken shops sell drumsticks with the skin already removed.

Boning a whole chicken is a technique used for special-occasion dishes. With bones removed, the chicken makes a meaty casing for a luxurious stuffing and the cooked chicken is much easier to carve or slice than a whole chicken. Chicken presented in this way is often served cold. Chicken wings can also be boned and stuffed, making an easy-to-eat appetiser or finger food for parties.

Marinating chicken gives it extra flavour and moisture. Marinades usually contain at least one acid ingredient, such as wine, vinegar, lemon juice or even yoghurt, to tenderise, plus other ingredients to flavour and colour the chicken.

Marinating is ideal to use in conjunction with quick-cooking methods. Frozen chicken should be thawed before marinating.

Place chicken in a shallow ceramic or glass (not metal) container and pour in the marinade. Stir well to make sure the chicken is well coated. Cover with plastic wrap and refrigerate, usually for at least two to eight hours, or preferably overnight, turning occasionally.

When ready to cook, drain the chicken and reserve the liquid (or discard, according to the particular recipe) for basting during cooking and for making a sauce to serve with the finished dish, but make sure any sauces are boiled before serving. Honey or sugar should be used sparingly in marinades as sweet mixtures easily scorch during cooking.

Cooking techniques

Chicken must always be eaten thoroughly cooked. To test when roasted, grilled or barbecued poultry is cooked, insert a skewer into the thickest part of the chicken (the thigh). If the juices run clear, the chicken is done. If they are still very pink, it is not. You can also test for doneness by twisting or jiggling the leg. If it moves easily in its socket, the chicken is cooked. Pan-fried, grilled or barbecued chicken is cooked when the meat is tender enough to fall easily off the bone when tested with a fork.

There are two basic cooking methods—using either dry heat or moist heat.

DRY HEAT: Cookery comprises oven roasting, barbecuing and grilling, stir-frying and pan-frying. With these methods, timing is important to prevent a tough, dry result.

MOIST HEAT: Cookery comprises braising, casseroling, pot roasting, poaching and steaming. The less tender cuts are ideal here because they benefit from the long, slow cooking process.

ROASTING: Stuff and truss the whole chicken if desired. Preheat the oven and have the chicken ready at room temperature. Use a shallow ovenproof pan that fits the chicken comfortably without squashing it in. Place the chicken on a wire rack in the pan and pour a little wine or water into the bottom of the pan, if liked, to prevent the chicken from drying out. Brush the chicken all over with melted butter or oil. If the breast is browning too quickly, cover loosely with a piece of aluminium foil. Cook the chicken according to the directions in the recipe, basting occasionally. After roasting, let the chicken rest for 10 minutes, covered loosely with foil, before carving.

BARBECUING: Allow plenty of time for the barbecue to heat up, so that the chicken is cooking over glowing coals rather than flames. The cooking time of the chicken will depend on the thickness of the chicken pieces. There is a tendency for the outside of the chicken to cook too quickly when it is barbecued. If this happens, move the pieces further away from the heat, or brown the outside and then continue cooking, wrapped in aluminium foil. Serve the chicken wrapped in foil to preserve the juices. Brush any unwrapped pieces of chicken with marinade, butter or oil during cooking to prevent them from drying out.

To roast, place the chicken on a rack in a baking dish and brush with melted butter or oil.

To barbecue, place the chicken on a preheated grill and brush with marinade.

STARTERS & SALADS

CHICKEN LARB IN BANANA BLOSSOM

SERVES 4

1 tablespoon vegetable oil

400 g (14 oz) minced (ground) chicken

4 tablespoons chicken stock

1 stem lemongrass, white part only, finely chopped

1 kaffir lime leaf, shredded (see Note)

1½ tablespoons fish sauce

4 tablespoons lime juice

2 spring onions (scallions), chopped

3 red Asian shallots, finely sliced

1 large handful coriander (cilantro) leaves, shredded

1 handful mint, shredded

1 small red chilli, seeded and finely chopped

4 banana blossom leaves, washed and dried (see Note), or crisp lettuce leaves

3 tablespoons crispy fried shallots, for garnish

lime wedges, to serve

1 **Heat a wok** over medium heat, add the oil and swirl to coat. Add the chicken and stir-fry for 3–4 minutes, or until well browned. Add the stock, lemongrass, kaffir lime leaf and 1 tablespoon of fish sauce and simmer for 5 minutes. Remove from the heat.

2 **Allow to cool,** then stir in the lime juice, remaining fish sauce, spring onion, shallots, coriander, mint and chilli. Spoon the mixture into the banana blossom leaves, garnish with crisp fried shallots and serve with lime wedges on the side.

Note: Kaffir lime leaves are available in Asian food stores. They are eaten shredded, not whole. Banana blossom leaves are used purely for decorative purposes in this recipe.

TOM YUM GAI

SERVES 4

1.25 litres (44 fl oz/5 cups) good-quality chicken stock
4 pieces fresh galangal (about 5 cm/2 inches long), or ginger
4 kaffir lime leaves, finely shredded
1 stem lemongrass, white part only, thickly sliced
4 tablespoons lime juice
3–4 teaspoons fish sauce
2 teaspoons red curry paste
350 g (12 oz) boneless, skinless chicken thigh fillets, chopped
1 small red chilli, finely sliced
12 button mushrooms, cut in half
1 handful coriander (cilantro) leaves
1 handful mint
3 spring onions (scallions), finely sliced

1 Bring the stock to the boil in a saucepan over high heat. Add the galangal, kaffir lime leaves and lemongrass and cook for 8 minutes. Reduce the heat and add the lime juice, fish sauce and curry paste. Stir and simmer for a further 2 minutes.

2 Add the chicken and cook for 8 minutes, or until cooked. Remove and set aside. Adjust the taste with a little extra lime juice and fish sauce, if necessary. Strain the broth through muslin (cheesecloth), and discard the pieces. Return the broth to the saucepan. Add the chilli, mushrooms and chicken pieces.

3 Serve the soup topped with the coriander, mint and spring onions.

MONEY BAGS

MAKES 20

1 dried shiitake mushroom

1 tablespoon vegetable oil

4 red Asian shallots, finely chopped

1 garlic clove, finely chopped

1 small red chilli, seeded and
finely chopped

2 teaspoons grated fresh ginger

125 g (4½ oz) minced (ground) chicken

1 teaspoon ground coriander

2 tablespoons chopped coriander
(cilantro) leaves

2 teaspoons fish sauce

20 x 8 cm (3¼ inch) won ton wrappers
(see Note)

20 chives

vegetable oil, for deep-frying

1 Soak the shiitake mushroom in hot water for 10 minutes. Drain. Discard the woody stem and finely slice the cap.

2 Heat the oil in a wok over medium heat and swirl to coat. Stir-fry the shallots, garlic, chilli and ginger until softened but not browned. Add the chicken and ground coriander and stir-fry until the meat changes colour. Stir in the coriander leaves, fish sauce and mushroom. Allow to cool.

3 Spread the won ton wrappers out on a board and put a heaped teaspoon of the mixture in the middle of each. Use a finger to lightly wet with water the outer circle around the meat mixture, but not to the outer edges. Gather the wrapper points up to form a pouch and press together firmly.

4 Wrap a chive strand twice around the top of each won ton to form a small bag. Tie the chives into a knot to hold secure and trim. Fill a wok one-third full of vegetable oil and heat to 190°C (375°F), or until a cube of bread dropped in the oil browns in 10 seconds. Deep-fry the money bags in batches for 30–60 seconds, or until crisp and golden brown. Drain on crumpled paper towels. Serve warm with a dipping sauce.

Note: This recipe can be easily doubled. Money bags are excellent finger food at parties. Won ton wrappers are available from Asian supermarkets.

DEEP-FRIED CHICKEN WRAPPED IN PANDANUS LEAVES

SERVES 4

500 g (1 lb 2 oz) boneless, skinless chicken thighs, cut into 3 cm (1¼ inch) cubes

2 tablespoons coconut cream

1–1½ tablespoons red curry paste

2 tablespoons chopped coriander (cilantro) leaves

2 garlic cloves, chopped

2 teaspoons fish sauce

1 tablespoon finely grated palm sugar (jaggery) or soft brown sugar

pandanus leaves, for wrapping

oil, for deep-frying

sweet chilli sauce, to serve

1 Put the chicken, coconut cream, curry paste, coriander, garlic, fish sauce and palm sugar in a bowl and mix well to dissolve the sugar. Cover with plastic wrap and marinate in the refrigerator for at least 2 hours, or preferably overnight.

2 Wrap each portion of chicken in a pandanus leaf. To do this, put the chicken in the middle of the leaf and tie the leaf around to enclose as if tying a knot. Cut the leaf down to shorten it and create a little parcel, then continue with the remaining pieces.

3 Half-fill a wok with oil and heat to 180°C (350°F), or until a cube of bread dropped in the oil browns in 15 seconds. Add the parcels in batches and cook for about 5–6 minutes, or until the chicken is cooked and the parcels feel firm. Drain well on crumpled paper towels and serve hot with sweet chilli sauce.

CHARGRILLED CHICKEN AND PINK GRAPEFRUIT SALAD

SERVES 4

4 x 200 g (7 oz) boneless, skinless
  chicken breasts

4 tablespoons olive oil

2 teaspoons balsamic vinegar

2 pink grapefruit

½ teaspoon dijon mustard

1½ tablespoons pickled pink
  peppercorns, drained and rinsed

1 tablespoon snipped chives

rocket (arugula) leaves, to serve

1   Place the chicken breasts between two sheets of plastic wrap and pound each one with a mallet or rolling pin until 1.5 cm (⅝ inch) thick. Put 2 tablespoons of the oil in a shallow dish with the vinegar, and season with salt and freshly ground pepper. Add the chicken breasts, swish them around to coat, then cover and marinate in the refrigerator for 15 minutes, turning once.

2   Preheat a barbecue grill plate to medium and brush lightly with oil. Drain the chicken and cook on the hotplate for 7–8 minutes, or until cooked through, turning once. Remove from the heat, allow to cool to room temperature, then cut the chicken into slices about 1 cm (½ inch) thick.

3   Peel the grapefruit, removing all the bitter white pith. Working over a bowl to catch the juices, cut the grapefruit into segments between the membrane, removing any seeds. Reserve 1 tablespoon of the captured grapefruit juice and whisk in the mustard and remaining oil to make a dressing. Add the peppercorns and chives and season to taste with salt and freshly ground pepper.

4   Arrange the rocket leaves on four serving plates and top with the chicken and grapefruit segments. Drizzle with the dressing and serve.

CHICKEN WINGS WITH YOGHURT TOMATO DIP

SERVES 4

12 chicken wings

MARINADE

2 tablespoons vegetable oil

2 tablespoons honey

2 tablespoons chermoula paste

1 tablespoon lemon juice

YOGHURT TOMATO DIP

250 g (9 oz/1 cup) Greek-style yoghurt

1 tomato, deseeded and finely chopped

¼ red onion, finely chopped

2 teaspoons chermoula paste (available in jars from supermarkets)

1 Remove the tips from the chicken wings and cut the wings in half through the joint.

2 Combine the marinade ingredients in a large non-metallic dish. Add chicken wings and toss well to coat evenly. Cover and marinate for several hours, or overnight.

3 Preheat the oven to 180°C (350°F/Gas 4). Line a large baking tray with foil. Drain the wings, reserving the marinade. Put the wings on a rack on the baking tray. Bake for about 45 minutes, or until cooked and golden brown. Brush with the reserved marinade two to three times during cooking.

4 To make the dip, combine all the ingredients in a bowl. Serve the warm chicken wings with the yoghurt dip.

THAI CHICKEN CAKES

MAKES 15

DIPPING SAUCE

115 g (4 oz/½ cup) caster (superfine) sugar

2 teaspoons rice wine vinegar

1 tablespoon sweet chilli sauce

½ small Lebanese (short) cucumber, seeded and diced

500 g (1 lb 2 oz) minced (ground) chicken

4 spring onions (scallions), chopped

2 garlic cloves, chopped

2 teaspoons green curry paste

4 kaffir lime leaves, shredded

1 very large handful coriander (cilantro) leaves

⅛ teaspoon lime oil (optional)

1 tablespoon fish sauce

3 tablespoons coconut cream

50 g (1¾ oz) snake (yard-long) beans, cut into 5 mm (¼ inch) slices

oil, for deep-frying

1   To make the dipping sauce, put the sugar and 125 ml (4 fl oz/½ cup) of water in a small saucepan and stir over low heat until the sugar has dissolved. Bring to the boil and cook for 5 minutes, or until thick and syrupy. Cool. Stir in the vinegar, sweet chilli sauce and cucumber.

2   Put the chicken, spring onion, garlic, curry paste, lime leaves, coriander, lime oil, fish sauce and coconut cream in a food processor and process until well combined. Fold in the beans. Using 2 tablespoons of mixture at a time, form into 15 patties.

3   Fill a wok one-third full of oil and heat to 180°C (350°F), or until a cube of bread dropped in the oil browns in 15 seconds. Deep-fry the chicken cakes in three batches for 2–3 minutes, or until lightly golden and cooked through. Drain on crumpled paper towels. Serve with the dipping sauce.

QUAIL WITH HERB BUTTER STUFFING AND SALAD

SERVES 4

4 large cleaned quail, at room temperature

100 g (3½ oz) unsalted butter, softened

2 tablespoons snipped chives

2 tablespoons finely chopped lemon thyme leaves

1 garlic clove, crushed

olive oil, for brushing

4 lime wedges

ROCKET (ARUGULA) SALAD

2 tablespoons olive oil

1 tablespoon balsamic vinegar

¼ teaspoon soft brown sugar

½ teaspoon wholegrain mustard

80 g (2¾ oz/2 cups) baby rocket (arugula) leaves

50 g (1¾ oz/⅓ cup) sun-dried (sun-blush) tomatoes, thinly sliced

2 tablespoons chopped roasted hazelnuts

1 **Using kitchen scissors,** cut each quail down both sides of the backbone. Turn the quails over, skin-side-up, and gently flatten the centre of the birds with the palm of your hand. Using paper towels, clean out the insides. Rinse well and pat dry with paper towels.

2 **In a bowl,** mix together the butter, chives, lemon thyme and garlic. Roughly divide the herb butter into four portions.

3 **Heat the grill** (broiler) to medium and line the grill tray with foil. Take a quail and gently loosen the skin over each breast with your finger. Slide a portion of the herb butter between the skin and breast, then repeat with the remaining birds. Put the quail on the grill tray, lightly brush with olive oil and season with salt and coarse black pepper. Grill for 5 minutes, then turn the birds over and grill for another 3 minutes, or until golden brown.

4 **While the quail** are cooking, make the rocket salad. Put the oil, vinegar, sugar and mustard in a small screw-top jar and shake until well combined. Put the rocket, tomato and hazelnuts in a bowl, add the dressing and toss well. Serve the warm quail with the lime wedges and salad.

MARINATED STUFFED CHICKEN WINGS

SERVES 4

8 large chicken wings

cornflour (cornstarch), for coating

vegetable oil, for deep-frying

2 spring onions (scallions), sliced on the diagonal

MARINADE

1½ tablespoons light soy sauce

1 tablespoon honey

2 teaspoons grated fresh ginger

2 garlic cloves, finely chopped

FILLING

180 g (6 oz) minced (ground) pork

60 g (2¼ oz/⅓ cup) chopped water chestnuts

2 tablespoons chopped coriander (cilantro) leaves

2 teaspoons cornflour (cornstarch)

3 teaspoons grated fresh ginger

2 garlic cloves, chopped

2 teaspoons oyster sauce

2 teaspoons light soy sauce

¼ teaspoon sesame oil

1 Prepare the chicken by cutting down the middle through the loose skin, slightly closer to the drumstick. Twist and break the joint between one small drumstick and the wing, then cut through the joint. Take the wing section and, using a small sharp knife, gently scrape the meat away from the bone, being careful not to break the skin. Pull the bone away and discard. Carefully remove the bone from the small drumsticks by scraping the meat away from the bone. Put all the chicken pieces in a large bowl.

2 To make the marinade, combine all the ingredients in a bowl. Add the chicken and mix well. Cover and leave to marinate for at least 1 hour, or preferably overnight.

3 To make the filling, combine all the ingredients. Gently spoon into the deboned wings and drumsticks, and lightly coat in the cornflour. Half-fill a wok with oil and heat to 170°C (325°F), or until a cube of bread dropped in the oil browns in 20 seconds. Add the chicken in batches and cook for 8 minutes, or until cooked through. Don't have the oil too hot, otherwise you will find the chicken will brown too quickly and the centre won't cook. Drain on crumpled paper towels.

4 Garnish with spring onion and serve with steamed rice and green vegetables.

CHICKEN AND GREEN BEAN SALAD

SERVES 4–6

400 g (14 oz) minced (ground) chicken

1 onion, finely chopped

3 garlic cloves, finely chopped

2 lemongrass stems, white part only, finely chopped

2 kaffir lime leaves, finely chopped

1 small red chilli, seeded and finely chopped

2 tablespoons peanut oil

1 tablespoon grated palm sugar (jaggery) or soft brown sugar

1 teaspoon ground turmeric

SALAD

500 g (1 lb 2 oz) green beans, trimmed and cut into 1 cm (½ inch) lengths

30 g (1 oz/½ cup) shredded coconut, toasted

4 garlic cloves, sliced

4 red Asian shallots, halved and sliced

2 large red chillies, seeded and sliced

1 makrut (kaffir lime) leaf, finely shredded

1 large handful coriander (cilantro) leaves

2 tablespoons peanut oil

2 teaspoons sesame oil

juice of 2 limes

2 teaspoons grated palm sugar (jaggery) or soft brown sugar

1–2 tablespoons fish sauce

1 **Put the chicken,** onion, garlic, lemongrass, lime leaves, chilli, oil, sugar and turmeric in a large bowl. Mix well to combine and season with salt and pepper. Lay a piece of foil on a flat surface and top with a sheet of baking paper. Place half the chicken mixture lengthways in the centre and roll up tightly to form a log shape. Repeat with the remaining mixture to make two logs.

2 **Place the parcels** in a single layer in a steamer and cover with a lid. Sit the steamer over a wok or saucepan of boiling water and steam for 20–25 minutes, or until the chicken is cooked through. Remove the parcels from the steamer and set aside to cool slightly.

3 **To make the salad,** place the beans in the same steamer and steam for 5 minutes. Refresh under cold water. Combine the coconut, garlic, shallots, chilli, lime leaf and coriander in a salad bowl. Unwrap the chicken and break up with a fork to its original minced form. Stir the chicken and beans through the salad mixture.

4 **Combine the peanut** and sesame oils, lime juice, sugar and fish sauce in a jug. Pour the dressing over the salad and toss to combine.

CHICKEN AND MANGO SALAD WITH HONEY DRESSING

SERVES 4

DRESSING

60 ml (2 fl oz/¼ cup) rice vinegar

2 tablespoons honey

3 cm (1¼ inch) piece ginger, chopped

60 ml (2 fl oz/¼ cup) grapeseed oil

1 teaspoon sesame oil

125 g (4½ oz) mixed Asian salad leaves

1 large mango, thinly sliced

125 g (4½ oz/1 cup) yellow or red
cherry tomatoes, halved

½ small red onion, sliced into
thin wedges

1 cold barbecued chicken, fat and skin
removed, meat shredded

30 g (1 oz/¾ cup) snow pea
(mangetout) sprouts, trimmed

2 teaspoons toasted sesame seeds

1 **To make the dressing,** put the vinegar, honey and ginger in a mini processor and whizz in 3-second bursts for 20 seconds, or until finely chopped. With the motor running, slowly pour in the oils and whizz for 20 seconds, or until thick and creamy.

2 **Arrange the salad** leaves on individual plates and top with the mango, tomatoes, onion, chicken and snow pea sprouts. Drizzle with the dressing and sprinkle with the sesame seeds. Serve immediately.

CHICKEN SKEWERS WITH SPICY CHILLI DIPPING SAUCE

SERVES 4

SAUCE

2 lemongrass stems, white part only, chopped

8 coriander (cilantro) roots including 10 cm (4 inch) stems, chopped

7 cm (2¾ inch) piece galangal or ginger, chopped

1 large red Asian shallot, chopped

2 garlic cloves, chopped

1 large green chilli, seeded and chopped

3 large tomatoes

1 tablespoon oil

60 ml (2 fl oz/¼ cup) fish sauce

25 g (1 oz/¼ cup) shaved palm sugar (jaggery) or soft brown sugar

2 teaspoons tamarind concentrate or 2 tablespoons lemon juice

2 tablespoons chopped coriander (cilantro) leaves

750 g (1 lb 10 oz) boneless, skinless chicken breast, cubed

canola oil spray or olive oil spray

1 **To make the sauce,** put the lemongrass, coriander roots and stems, galangal, shallot, garlic and chilli in a small processor fitted with the metal blade. Whizz in 3–4-second bursts for 30 seconds, or until finely chopped.

2 **Score a cross** in the base of each tomato. Put in a heatproof bowl and cover with boiling water. Leave for 30 seconds, then transfer to cold water and peel the skin away from the cross. Roughly chop the tomatoes.

3 **Heat the oil** in a large heavy-based saucepan. Add the lemongrass paste, stir, then add two-thirds of the chopped tomato. Cook, stirring, for 5 minutes. Set aside to cool slightly, then transfer to the processor and whizz for 15 seconds, or until smooth. Add the remaining tomato and whizz in short bursts for 15 seconds, or until the mixture is finely chopped but still has texture.

4 **Return the mixture** to the saucepan and add the fish sauce, sugar and tamarind concentrate. Simmer, stirring frequently, for 10 minutes. Stir in the coriander leaves.

5 **Thread the chicken** onto metal skewers and spray with oil. Preheat the barbecue or chargrill pan to high and cook the chicken, turning frequently, for 5–7 minutes, or until just cooked through. Serve immediately, accompanied by the sauce.

CRUNCHY PARCEL CHICKEN SALAD WITH REMOULADE

SERVES 4

2 skinless, boneless chicken breasts (about 300 g/10½ oz each)

1 red onion, finely diced

1 tablespoon roughly chopped oregano

1 teaspoon dried oregano

2 tablespoons olive oil

REMOULADE

185 g (6½ oz/¾ cup) whole-egg mayonnaise

2 teaspoons dijon mustard

1 tablespoon capers, rinsed and squeezed dry, chopped

25 g (1 oz) cornichons, finely diced

1 tablespoon finely snipped chives

1 garlic clove, crushed

1 tablespoon lime juice

1 tablespoon chopped flat-leaf (Italian) parsley

CRUNCHY SALAD

2 iceberg lettuce hearts, shredded

2 celery stalks, finely sliced on the diagonal

2 green apples, peeled, cored and cut into thin matchsticks

4 radishes, trimmed and cut into thin matchsticks

100 g (3½ oz/1 cup) walnuts, toasted and halved

1 **Preheat the oven** to 180°C (350°F/Gas 4). Pat dry the chicken breasts with paper towels, then place each breast on a piece of baking paper large enough to wrap the breast and its topping. Combine the onion and fresh and dried oregano in a bowl and season to taste. Lightly rub the olive oil onto each breast then cover evenly with the herb mixture. Fold the baking paper over each chicken breast, then tuck the ends underneath so it is secure. Cover each parcel with foil to help retain the juices and place in a roasting tin. Bake for about 25–30 minutes, or until cooked through. Rest for 5 minutes before opening the parcels.

2 **To make the remoulade,** combine all the ingredients in a bowl and season. Cover and refrigerate until ready to serve.

3 **Combine the salad ingredients** in a bowl and toss with the remoulade.

4 **Remove the chicken breasts** from the parcels and finely slice. Arrange the slices over each plated salad. This is delicious served with crusty bread.

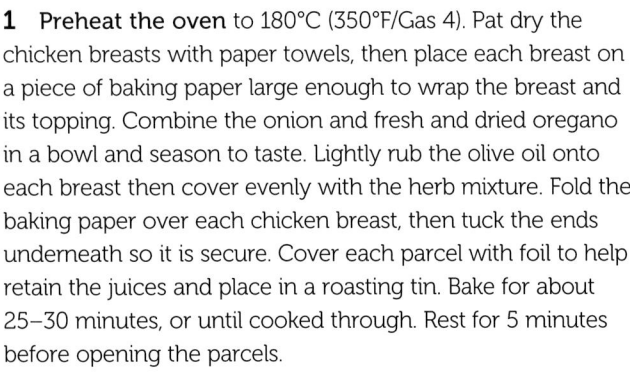

CHICKEN SATAY

SERVES 4

1 tablespoon mild curry powder

1 tablespoon fish sauce

1 tablespoon shaved palm sugar (jaggery) or soft brown sugar

2 garlic cloves, roughly chopped

1 tablespoon chopped coriander (cilantro) stems

80 ml (2½ fl oz/⅓ cup) oil

12 chicken tenderloins

1 small handful coriander (cilantro) leaves

2–3 tablespoons fried shallots

SATAY SAUCE

1 tablespoon tamarind pulp (available from Asian supermarkets)

125 ml (4 fl oz/½ cup) boiling water

350 g (12 oz/2¼ cups) roasted peanuts

500 ml (17 fl oz/2 cups) coconut cream

1 tablespoon red curry paste

1 tablespoon shaved palm sugar (jaggery) or soft brown sugar

1 tablespoon kecap manis (Indonesian soy sauce)

2 tablespoons fish sauce

1 tablespoon lime juice

1 kaffir lime leaf

½–2 teaspoons chilli sauce, to taste

1 Combine the curry powder, fish sauce, sugar, garlic, coriander stems and oil in a mini processor and whizz for 40 seconds, or until smooth. Thread each chicken tenderloin onto a bamboo skewer and place in a shallow ceramic or glass dish. Pour the marinade over the skewers, turning to coat the chicken. Cover and chill for 3–4 hours, or overnight.

2 To make the satay sauce, put the tamarind pulp in a heatproof bowl, add the boiling water and soak for 30 minutes. Mash the pulp with a fork and strain the liquid through a fine sieve. Reserve the liquid and discard the pulp.

3 Put the peanuts in a small processor fitted with the metal blade and whizz until roughly ground (don't chop the nuts too finely as some texture is desirable). Add the coconut cream, curry paste, sugar, kecap manis, fish sauce, lime juice and 2 tablespoons of tamarind water. Whizz for 1–2 minutes, or until well combined. Transfer to a wok or large saucepan.

4 Add the lime leaf to the peanut mixture and bring to the boil over medium heat. Stir in the chilli sauce, to taste. Reduce the heat to low and simmer, stirring often, for 10 minutes, being careful not to let it boil or the coconut cream may split.

5 Preheat the barbecue or chargrill pan to high. Cook the chicken skewers, turning several times, for 5 minutes, or until cooked through.

6 Arrange the chicken skewers on a platter, sprinkle the coriander and fried shallots on top and spoon over the warm satay sauce.

POACHED CHICKEN SALAD WITH HOKKIEN NOODLES

SERVES 4

450 g (1 lb) boneless, skinless chicken breast

6 cm (2½ inch) piece fresh ginger

6 whole allspice

½ teaspoon coriander seeds

400 g (14 oz) hokkien (egg) noodles

160 g (5¾ oz/1½ cups) snake (yard-long) beans, sliced diagonally lengthways

115 g (4 oz/⅔) baby corn, cut in half lengthways

100 g (3½ oz/1 cup) snow peas (mangetout), trimmed and finely shredded lengthways

½ large green chilli, deseeded and finely sliced (optional)

1 large handful mint

1 handful coriander (cilantro) leaves

DRESSING

2 tablespoons tamari

juice of 1 lime

1 tablespoon sesame oil

2 teaspoons soft brown sugar

1 Put the chicken, ginger, whole allspice and coriander seeds into a saucepan, cover with water, and bring to the boil over medium heat. Reduce the heat, and simmer for 12 minutes, or until the chicken is cooked. Allow to cool slightly, then remove and finely slice the chicken.

2 Place the noodles in a large heatproof bowl and cover with boiling water. Stand for a few minutes, until the noodles soften slightly, then separate with a fork and drain well.

3 Put the chicken, beans, corn, snow peas, chilli, mint, coriander and combined dressing ingredients in a bowl, and toss lightly.

4 Divide the noodles among four serving plates. Top with salad and serve immediately.

CHICKEN IN PANDANUS LEAVES

MAKES 20

2 garlic cloves, crushed

2 cm (¾ inch) piece fresh ginger, peeled
 and chopped

1 small onion, chopped

1 stem lemongrass, white part only,
 sliced

1 tablespoon fish sauce

2 tablespoons kecap manis (see Note)

1 tablespoon worcestershire sauce

125 ml (4 fl oz/½ cup) coconut milk

2 teaspoons grated palm sugar or
 soft brown sugar

500 g (1 lb 2 oz) boneless, skinless
 chicken thighs, cut into
 20 large chunks

20 pandanus leaves (see Note)

DIPPING SAUCE

125 ml (4 fl oz/½ cup) white vinegar

3 tablespoons shaved palm sugar
 (jaggery) or soft brown sugar

1 tablespoon dark soy sauce

1 teaspoon toasted sesame seeds

1 **Put the garlic,** ginger, onion, lemongrass, fish sauce, kecap manis, worcestershire sauce and ¼ teaspoon of pepper in a food processor and blend to a smooth paste. Gradually blend in the coconut milk and sugar.

2 **Transfer the paste** to a shallow non-metallic dish, add the chicken and combine well. Cover with plastic wrap and refrigerate for 2 hours.

3 **Put the dipping** sauce ingredients in a bowl and stir until the sugar has dissolved. Set aside until needed.

4 **Preheat a barbecue grill** plate or flat plate to medium. Trim the pandanus leaves into strips about 15 cm (6 inches) long. Put a piece of chicken on each leaf, then roll each one up tightly and secure with a toothpick to make 20 parcels.

5 **Put the parcels** on a lightly oiled hotplate and cook for 5–6 minutes on each side, or until the chicken is cooked through. Serve hot with the dipping sauce.

Note: Instead of kecap manis, you can use soy sauce with a little soft brown sugar mixed in it. Fresh pandanus leaves are available from Asian grocery stores. They impart a floral flavour to cooked dishes but are not edible themselves.

CHICKEN PHO

2.5 litres (87 fl oz/10 cups) chicken stock

8 black peppercorns

2 cm (¾ inch) piece fresh ginger, sliced

1 onion, thinly sliced

3 tablespoons crisp fried shallots
(see Note)

1–1½ tablespoons fish sauce

1 boneless, skinless chicken breast,
trimmed

500 g (1 lb 2 oz) fresh round rice
noodles

3 tablespoons chopped coriander
(cilantro) leaves

90 g (3¼ oz/1 cup) bean sprouts,
tails trimmed

3 tablespoons Vietnamese mint

3 tablespoons Thai basil

2 small red chillies, sliced

lime wedges, to serve

1 Put the stock in a wok with 125 ml (4 fl oz/½ cup) of water, the peppercorns, ginger, onion, crisp fried shallots, fish sauce and ½ teaspoon of salt. Bring to the boil over high heat, then reduce the heat so the stock is just simmering and cook for 5 minutes. Put the chicken breast in the stock and gently poach for 12–15 minutes, or until just cooked through and tender. Remove the chicken, shred and set aside. Strain the stock, then return it to a clean wok and bring to a simmer.

2 Put the noodles in a heatproof bowl and cover with boiling water. Gently separate them, then drain and rinse under cold water and divide among four serving bowls. Top the noodles with the shredded chicken, then ladle on the stock. Garnish with the chopped coriander, bean sprouts, mint, basil and chilli slices. Serve with lime wedges on the side.

Note: Crisp fried shallots are available at Asian supermarkets.

CHICKEN AND COCONUT RICE IN BANANA LEAVES

MAKES ABOUT 12

2–3 young banana leaves or squares of aluminium foil

400 g (14 oz/2 cups) glutinous white rice

185 ml (6 fl oz/¾ cup) coconut milk

CHICKEN FILLING

2 tablespoons oil

2–3 garlic cloves, crushed

6 curry leaves

1 teaspoon shrimp paste

2 teaspoons ground coriander

2 teaspoons ground cumin

½ teaspoon ground turmeric

250 g (9 oz) minced (ground) chicken

3 tablespoons coconut milk

1 teaspoon lemon juice

1 **With a sharp knife,** cut away the central ribs of the banana leaves. The leaves will split into large pieces — cut these into 15 cm (6 inch) squares. Blanch in boiling water briefly to soften them, then spread out on a tea towel (dish cloth) and cover.

2 **Wash and drain** the rice, then put it in a large heavy-based saucepan with 435 ml (15¼ fl oz/1¾ cups) of water. Bring slowly to the boil, then reduce the heat to very low, cover tightly and cook for 15 minutes.

3 **Put the coconut milk** and 125 ml (4 fl oz/½ cup) of water in a small saucepan and heat without boiling. Pour over the rice and stir through with a fork. Transfer to a bowl and set aside to cool.

4 **To make the filling,** heat the oil in a large heavy-based frying pan over medium heat, add the garlic and curry leaves and stir for 1 minute. Add the dried shrimp paste, coriander, cumin and turmeric and cook for another minute. Add the chicken and cook, breaking up with a fork, for 3–4 minutes, or until the chicken changes colour. Pour in the coconut milk and cook over low heat for 5 minutes, or until absorbed. Remove the curry leaves. Add the lemon juice and season with salt and pepper, to taste. Leave to cool.

5 **Place** 1 heaped tablespoon of rice in the centre of each piece of banana leaf and flatten to a 4 cm (1½ inch) square. Top with a heaped teaspoon of filling. Roll the leaf into a parcel and place, seam side down, in a steamer lined with leftover banana leaf scraps (you may have to do this in batches). Cover with a lid, sit the steamer over a wok or saucepan of boiling water and steam for 15 minutes. Serve at room temperature with chopsticks or small forks.

VIETNAMESE-STYLE CHICKEN AND CABBAGE SALAD

SERVES 4

3 boneless, skinless chicken breasts,
  cut into 1 cm (½ inch) thick slices

1 red chilli, seeded and finely chopped

3 tablespoons lime juice

2 tablespoons grated palm sugar
  (jaggery) or soft brown sugar

3 tablespoons fish sauce

½ Chinese cabbage, shredded

2 carrots, grated

1 large handful mint, shredded

1 **Line a steamer** with baking paper and punch with holes. Arrange the chicken slices on top and cover with a lid. Sit the steamer over a wok or saucepan of boiling water and steam for about 10 minutes, or until cooked through. Cool, then shred into small pieces.

2 **Combine the chilli,** lime juice, sugar and fish sauce.

3 **Combine the chicken,** cabbage, carrot, mint and dressing in a bowl. Toss well and serve immediately.

SAKE-STEAMED CHICKEN SALAD

SERVES 4

250 ml (9 fl oz/1 cup) cooking sake (see Note)

100 ml (3½ fl oz/½ cups) chicken or vegetable stock

5 cm (2 inch) piece ginger, grated

2 garlic cloves, crushed

6 coriander (cilantro) roots, washed well

4 black peppercorns, cracked

2 bay leaves

600 g (1 lb 5 oz) boneless, skinless chicken breast, cut into thin strips

75 g (2½ oz/2 cups) watercress, trimmed, or 100 g (3½ oz) other salad leaves

3 spring onions (scallions), sliced

CORIANDER (CILANTRO) DRESSING

4 tablespoons olive oil

1 tablespoon red or white wine vinegar

2 tablespoons chopped coriander (cilantro) leaves

2 tablespoons chopped flat-leaf (Italian) parsley

1   Combine the sake, stock, ginger, garlic, coriander roots, peppercorns and bay leaves in a jug. Put the chicken strips in a heatproof shallow dish that fits into a large steamer and pour the sauce over the chicken. Toss to mix well.

2   Put the dish in the steamer and cover with a lid. Sit the steamer over a wok or saucepan of boiling water and steam for 20–25 minutes, or until the chicken is cooked through, turning the chicken a couple of times during cooking to prevent it all sticking together. Remove the chicken from the liquid, reserving the liquid.

3   Meanwhile, to make the dressing, combine the oil and vinegar with 3 tablespoons of the cooking liquid and whisk well to combine. Add the coriander and parsley and season with salt and freshly ground black pepper. Spoon half of the dressing over the chicken, mix well, then leave to cool.

4   Put the chicken and watercress in a bowl, drizzle with the remaining dressing and scatter the spring onion over the top.

Note: Cooking sake is less expensive than regular sake. It is available from Asian food stores or the Asian section of larger supermarkets.

BABY COS VIETNAMESE CHICKEN CUPS

MAKES 8

300 g (10½ oz) boneless, skinless
chicken breast

4 spring onions (scallions), finely sliced

1 large handful coriander
(cilantro) leaves

1 handful mint, torn

1 ripe but firm mango, flesh cut into
thin strips

1 Lebanese (short) cucumber, seeded
and cut into thin strips

2 tablespoons toasted peanuts

2 tablespoons fried shallots (see Note)

2 baby cos (romaine) lettuces, gently
separated into 8 cups and rinsed

DRESSING

1 garlic clove, crushed

1 large red chilli, seeded and
finely chopped

1 lemongrass stem, white part only,
finely chopped

1 tablespoon grated fresh ginger

2 tablespoons lime juice

2 tablespoons fish sauce

2 teaspoons caster (superfine) sugar

1 Line the base of a steamer with baking paper and punch with holes. Place the chicken in the steamer in a single layer and cover securely with a lid. Sit the steamer over a wok or saucepan of boiling water and steam for 5–7 minutes, or until cooked when tested with a skewer. Remove the chicken and set aside on a plate to cool.

2 Put the spring onion, coriander, mint, mango, cucumber, peanuts and fried shallots in a large bowl. Shred the cooled chicken and add to the mixture.

3 To make the dressing, combine the garlic, chilli, lemongrass, ginger, lime juice, fish sauce, sugar and 1 tablespoon of water in a bowl and whisk until sugar has dissolved. Pour the dressing over the chicken mixture and toss it through.

4 Spoon heaped tablespoons of the chicken mixture into each lettuce cup and serve immediately.

Note: Fried shallots are available from Asian food shops or in the Asian section of larger supermarkets.

CHICKEN AND PISTACHIO DUMPLINGS

MAKES 20

300 g (10½ oz) minced (ground) chicken

80 g (2¾ oz/½ cup) unsalted pistachio nuts, finely chopped

1 garlic clove, crushed

2 tablespoons chopped mint

1 tablespoon grated lemon zest

½ teaspoon ground allspice

¼ teaspoon ground cinnamon

¼ teaspoon Tabasco sauce

20 round gow gee dumpling wrappers (available in Asian supermarkets)

SAUCE

1 tablespoon olive oil

1 small onion, finely chopped

1 red chilli, seeded and finely chopped

2 garlic cloves, crushed

3 tablespoons dry white wine

400 g (14 oz) tin chopped tomatoes

1 cinnamon stick

½ teaspoon Tabasco sauce (optional)

1 **Combine the chicken,** pistachios, garlic, mint, lemon zest, allspice, cinnamon, Tabasco, ¼ teaspoon of ground black pepper and some salt in a bowl. Spoon the mixture in the centre of the gow gee wrappers and bring the edges up around the filling, pleating as you go to encase the filling (leave the top open).

2 **Line a steamer** with baking paper and punch with holes. Place the dumplings in a single layer on top and cover with a lid. Sit the steamer over a wok or saucepan of boiling water and steam for 15 minutes, or until cooked. If the dumplings start to dry out during cooking, brush generously with water.

3 **To make** the sauce, heat the oil in a small saucepan over medium heat. Add the onion, chilli and garlic and cook, stirring, for 5 minutes, or until the onion has softened. Add the wine, tomatoes, cinnamon and Tabasco, bring to the boil, then reduce the heat and simmer, stirring occasionally, for about 15 minutes. Remove the cinnamon stick and transfer the sauce to a food processor. Blend until smooth, then season well.

4 **To serve,** spoon the sauce onto serving plates and place the dumplings on top, or arrange the dumplings on a platter and use the sauce for dipping.

SMOKED CHICKEN CAESAR SALAD

SERVES 4

GARLIC CROUTONS
1 thin baguette

45 g (1½ oz) unsalted butter

125 ml (4 fl oz/½ cup) olive oil

4 garlic cloves, crushed

1 cos (romaine) lettuce, tough outer
  leaves discarded

1 large smoked chicken (about
  950 g/1 lb 14 oz)

150 g (5 oz/ 1½ cups) parmesan cheese
  shavings

DRESSING
2 eggs

2 garlic cloves, crushed

2 tablespoons lemon juice

2 teaspoons dijon mustard

45 g (1½ oz) can anchovy fillets, drained

250 ml (9 fl oz/ 1 cup) olive oil

¼ teaspoon salt

1 teaspoon freshly ground black pepper

1 **To make croutons,** slice the baguette diagonally into
1 cm (½ inch) thick slices. Melt the butter and olive oil in a
large frying pan over moderate heat. Stir in the crushed garlic.
Fry the bread slices, a few at a time, until golden. Remove from
the pan and drain on paper towels.

2 **Separate lettuce leaves,** wash and dry thoroughly. Tear the
larger leaves into pieces and refrigerate until well chilled. Cut
the chicken into bite-sized chunks. Refrigerate while preparing
the dressing.

3 **To make dressing,** blend or process the eggs, garlic,
lemon juice, mustard and anchovies. With the motor running,
gradually pour in the oil in a thin stream and process until
thick. Season with the salt and pepper.

4 **In a large bowl,** combine the torn lettuce leaves, chicken,
about half of the croutons and half the parmesan cheese. Add
the dressing and toss well. Arrange 2–3 whole lettuce leaves in
each individual serving bowl, spoon in the salad and sprinkle
with the remaining croutons and parmesan. Season liberally
with freshly ground black pepper and serve immediately.

CHICKEN, PANCETTA AND PINE NUT TERRINES

SERVES 10

125 g (4½ oz) piece pancetta, diced

60 g (2¼ oz) unsalted butter, softened

1 onion, finely chopped

300 g (10½ oz) boneless, skinless chicken breasts, roughly chopped

2 tablespoons brandy

80 ml (2½ fl oz/⅓ cup) thick (double/heavy) cream

25 g (1 oz/⅓ cup) fresh breadcrumbs

2 tablespoons chopped tarragon

40 g (1½ oz/¼ cup) toasted pine nuts

slices of baguette, to serve

capers, to serve

extra tarragon sprigs, to serve

1 Grease 10 small ramekins.

2 Heat a frying pan over high heat for 2 minutes, or until hot, add the pancetta and stir-fry for 3–4 minutes, or until the pancetta is lightly browned and the fat has rendered. Add half the butter and reduce the heat to low. Add the onion and fry gently for 5 minutes, or until softened. Add the chicken and cook for 5 minutes. Stir in the brandy, cover and cook for 3 minutes, or until the chicken is cooked through.

3 Transfer mixture to a small processor fitted with the metal blade. Add the remaining butter, the cream, breadcrumbs, tarragon and pine nuts and whizz for 8 seconds, or until roughly chopped. Spoon the mixture into the prepared ramekins, pressing down firmly and smoothing the surface. Refrigerate for 4 hours, or until firm to the touch.

4 Invert the terrines onto serving plates and serve with baguette slices, garnished with capers and tarragon.

Note: The terrine mixture can also be set in a loaf (bar) tin and served in slices.

CHICKEN SANDWICH

SERVES 4

2 boneless skinless chicken breasts,
  cut in half horizontally

2 tablespoons olive oil

2 tablespoons lemon juice

4 large pieces ciabatta or Turkish bread,
  cut in half horizontally

1 garlic clove, cut in half

mayonnaise

1 avocado, sliced

2 tomatoes, sliced

a large handful of rocket (arugula)
  leaves, long stems snapped off

1 Flatten each piece of chicken by hitting it either with your fist, the flat side of a knife blade or cleaver, or with a meat mallet. Don't break the flesh, just thin it out a bit. Trim off any fat or sinew.

2 Heat the oil in a frying pan, add the chicken pieces and fry them on both sides for a couple of minutes, or until they turn brown and are cooked through (you can check by cutting into the middle of one). Sprinkle with the lemon juice, then take the chicken out of the pan. Add the bread to the pan with the cut-side down and cook for a minute, pressing down on it to flatten it and help soak up any juices.

3 Take the bread out of the pan, rub the cut side of the garlic over the surface, then spread all the pieces with a generous amount of mayonnaise.

4 Put a piece of chicken on four of the pieces, season and then layer with the avocado and tomato, seasoning as you go. Finish with the rocket and the tops of the bread, then serve.

SPINACH SALAD WITH CHICKEN AND SESAME DRESSING

SERVES 4

450 g (1 lb) baby English spinach leaves

1 Lebanese (short) cucumber, peeled and diced

4 spring onions (scallions), shredded

2 carrots, cut into matchsticks

2 chicken breasts, cooked

2 tablespoons tahini paste

2 tablespoons lime juice

3 teaspoons sesame oil

1 teaspoon sugar

pinch of chilli flakes

2 tablespoons sesame seeds

a large handful coriander (cilantro) leaves

1 **Put the spinach** in a large bowl. Scatter the cucumber, spring onion and carrot over the top. Shred the chicken breast into long pieces and scatter it over the vegetables.

2 **Combine the tahini,** lime juice, sesame oil, sugar and chilli flakes, then add salt to taste. Drizzle this dressing over the salad.

3 **Cook sesame seeds** in a dry frying pan over low heat for a minute or two, stirring them around. When they start to brown and smell toasted, tip them over the salad. Scatter the coriander leaves over the top. Toss the salad just before serving.

VIETNAMESE CHICKEN SALAD

SERVES 4

2 chicken breasts or 4 chicken thighs,
    cooked

2 tablespoons lime juice

1½ tablespoons fish sauce

¼ teaspoon sugar

1–2 bird's eye chillies, finely chopped

1 garlic clove, crushed

2 French shallots, finely sliced

2 handfuls bean sprouts

a large handful shredded
    Chinese cabbage

4 tablespoons Vietnamese mint or mint
    leaves, finely chopped

1 **Take the flesh off** the chicken bones and shred it. Discard the skin and bones.

2 **Combine the lime juice,** fish sauce, sugar, chilli, garlic and shallot.

3 **Bring a saucepan** of water to the boil and throw in the bean sprouts. After 10 seconds, drain them and rinse under cold water to stop them cooking any longer.

4 **Mix the bean sprouts** with the Chinese cabbage, Vietnamese mint and chicken. Pour the dressing over the salad and toss everything together well.

Note: Wear rubber gloves when chopping the chillies. Their heat can burn your skin. Discard seeds for a milder taste.

LEMPER

MAKES 20

COCONUT RICE

500 g (1 lb 2 oz/2½ cups) glutinous white rice, soaked in cold water for 30 minutes

250 ml (9 fl oz/1 cup) coconut cream

FILLING

2 tablespoons peanut oil

1 small red chilli, seeded and finely chopped

4 garlic cloves, finely chopped

3–4 red Asian shallots, finely chopped

1 stem lemongrass, white part only, finely chopped

4 fresh curry leaves, crushed

2 teaspoons ground coriander

2 teaspoons ground cumin

1 teaspoon shrimp paste

300 g (10½ oz) minced (ground) chicken

white pepper, to taste

2 teaspoons lemon juice

2 banana leaves

1 **Rinse the rice** under cold running water. Put the rice and 500 ml (17 fl oz/2 cups) of water in a large saucepan, bring to the boil and cover with a tight-fitting lid. Reduce the heat and simmer for 15 minutes. Add 185 ml (6 fl oz/¾ cup) of the coconut cream and 125 ml (4 fl oz/½ cup) of water and stir well. Cover and continue to cook over very low heat for 5–10 minutes, or until the liquid is absorbed. Remove from the heat and leave with the lid on for about 10 minutes.

2 **To make** the filling, heat a wok over medium heat, add the oil and swirl to coat. Add the chilli, garlic, shallots, lemongrass and curry leaves and stir-fry for 1 minute, or until fragrant. Add the coriander, cumin and shrimp paste, and cook for another minute, stirring in the shrimp paste until it is well combined. Add the chicken and stir-fry for 3 minutes, or until it changes colour. Pour in the remaining coconut cream and cook over low heat for 10 minutes, or until mixture is quite dry. Season

with salt and white pepper; drizzle with the lemon juice. Cool on a lined baking tray. Divide into 20 portions.

3 **Wash banana leaves** in warm water. Cut them down the centre to remove the rib, then cut into 14 x 8 cm (5½ x 3¼ inch) rectangles. You may need to soak them in hot water to make them pliable but make sure they are dry before using them to wrap the rice. Spread a portion of rice to 1 cm (½ inch) thick over each rectangle, leaving a 5 mm (¼ inch) border on each end. Put 1 tablespoon of the chicken mixture in the centre of the rice and roll into a cylinder, securing with kitchen string or a toothpick.

4 **Put a single layer** of lemper seam side down in a bamboo steamer and place over a wok of simmering water and steam for 5 minutes. Repeat with remaining lemper. Or, use stacks of steamers, swap them halfway through and cook for about 2 minutes longer. Serve at room temperature.

CHILLI CHICKEN AND CASHEW SALAD

SERVES 4

3 tablespoons sweet chilli sauce

2 tablespoons lime juice

2 teaspoons fish sauce

2 tablespoons chopped coriander
(cilantro)

1 garlic clove, crushed

1 small red chilli, finely chopped

1½ teaspoons grated fresh ginger

2 tablespoons olive oil

600 g (1 lb 5 oz) boneless, skinless
chicken breasts

100 g (3½ oz) salad leaves

250 g (9 oz/1½ cups) cherry tomatoes,
halved

100 g (3½ oz) Lebanese (short)
cucumber, cut into bite-sized chunks

50 g (1¾/½ cup) snow pea (mangetout)
sprouts, trimmed

80 g (2¾ oz/½ cup) cashew nuts,
roughly chopped

1 Combine chilli sauce, lime juice, fish sauce, coriander, garlic, chilli, ginger and 1 tablespoon of the oil in a large bowl.

2 Heat remaining oil in a frying or chargrill pan over medium heat until hot, and cook the chicken for 5–8 minutes on each side or until cooked through. While still hot, slice each breast widthways into 1 cm slices and toss in the bowl with the dressing. Leave to cool slightly.

3 Combine salad leaves, cherry tomatoes, cucumber chunks and snow pea sprouts in a serving bowl. Add the chicken and all of the dressing, and toss gently until the leaves are lightly coated. Scatter with chopped cashews and serve.

CHICKEN AND PASTA SALAD WITH MUSTARD DRESSING

SERVES 4

1 tablespoon balsamic vinegar

150 ml (5 fl oz) olive oil

1 tablespoon lemon juice

3 tablespoons wholegrain mustard

200 g (7 oz) bucatini

450 g (1 lb) good-quality smoked
chicken breast

8 small radishes

2 small eating apples

4 spring onions, (scallions) finely sliced

35 g (1¼ oz/1 cup) rocket (arugula)

1   Combine the vinegar, olive oil, lemon juice and mustard in a screw-top jar, and shake well to combine. Season to taste with salt and pepper. Bring a large saucepan of salted water to the boil. Cook the bucatini according to the packet instructions until al dente. Drain, rinse under cold water and drain again. Toss one-third of the dressing through the bucatini and set aside for 30 minutes.

2   Cut the chicken breast on the diagonal and place in a large bowl. Thinly slice the radishes and add to the chicken. Quarter, core and cube the apples without peeling them, and add to the chicken with the sliced spring onion and rocket. Pour in the remaining dressing and toss lightly.

3   Gently mix the pasta with the smoked chicken until well combined. Divide the salad among four serving dishes and serve with fresh, crusty bread. May be served cold as a light meal or entrée.

Note: Bucatini is a thick, spaghetti-like pasta with a hollow centre. It has a chewy texture. Smoked chicken often has a dark skin. You may wish to remove this to improve the appearance of the salad.

WARM CHICKEN AND PASTA SALAD

SERVES 4

375 g (13 oz) penne

100 ml (3½ fl oz) olive oil

4 long, thin eggplants (aubergines), thinly sliced on the diagonal

2 boneless, skinless chicken breasts

2 teaspoons lemon juice

1 large handful chopped flat-leaf (Italian) parsley

270 g (9½ oz) chargrilled red capsicum (pepper), drained and sliced (see Note)

155 g (5½ oz) fresh asparagus spears, trimmed, blanched and cut into 5 cm lengths

85 g (3 oz) semi-dried (sun-blushed) tomatoes, finely sliced

grated parmesan cheese (optional)

1 Cook the pasta in a large saucepan of boiling water until al dente. Drain, return to the pan and keep warm. Heat 2 tablespoons of the oil in a large frying pan over high heat and cook the eggplant for 4–5 minutes, or until golden and cooked through.

2 Heat a lightly oiled chargrill pan over high heat and cook the chicken for 5 minutes each side, or until browned and cooked through. Cut into thick slices. Combine the lemon juice, parsley and the remaining oil in a small jar and shake well. Return the pasta to the heat, toss through the dressing, chicken, eggplant, capsicum, asparagus and tomato until well mixed and warmed through. Season with black pepper. Serve warm with a scattering of grated parmesan, if desired.

Note: Jars of chargrilled capsicum are available from supermarkets and delicatessens.

INDIAN MARINATED CHICKEN SALAD

SERVES 4

60 ml (2 fl oz/¼ cup) lemon juice

1½ teaspoons garam masala

1 teaspoon ground turmeric

1 tablespoon finely grated fresh ginger

2 garlic cloves, finely chopped

3½ tablespoons vegetable oil

650 g (1 lb 7oz) boneless, skinless
chicken breast

1 onion, thinly sliced

2 zucchini (courgettes), thinly sliced
on the diagonal

100 g (3½ oz/3 cups) watercress leaves

150 g (5½ oz/1 cup) freshly shelled peas

2 ripe tomatoes, finely chopped

1 large handful coriander (cilantro)
leaves

DRESSING

1 teaspoon cumin seeds

½ teaspoon coriander seeds

90 g (3¼ oz/⅓ cup) plain yoghurt

2 tablespoons chopped mint

2 tablespoons lemon juice

1   Combine the lemon juice, garam masala, turmeric, ginger, garlic and 2 teaspoons oil in a large bowl. Add the chicken breasts and onion, toss to coat in the marinade, cover, and refrigerate for 1 hour.

2   Discard the onion, then heat 2 tablespoons of oil in a large frying pan. Cook the chicken for about 4–5 minutes on each side or until it is cooked through. Remove the chicken from the pan and leave for 5 minutes. Cut each breast across the grain into 1 cm (½ inch) slices.

3   Heat the remaining oil in the pan and cook the zucchini for 2 minutes, or until lightly golden and tender. Toss with the watercress in a large bowl. Cook the peas in boiling water for 5 minutes, or until tender, then drain. Rinse under cold water to cool. Add to the salad with the tomato, chicken and coriander.

4   For the dressing, gently roast the cumin and coriander seeds in a dry frying pan for 1–2 minutes, or until fragrant. Remove, then pound the seeds to a powder. Mix with the yoghurt, mint and lemon juice, then gently fold through the salad.

SOUPS

CREAMY CHICKEN AND CORN SOUP

SERVES 4–6

20 g (¾ oz) butter

1 tablespoon olive oil

500 g (1 lb 2 oz) boneless, skinless
   chicken thighs, trimmed and
   thinly sliced

2 garlic cloves, chopped

1 leek, chopped

1 large celery stalk, chopped

1 bay leaf

½ teaspoon thyme

1 litre (35 fl oz/4 cups) chicken stock

60 ml (2 fl oz/¼ cup) sherry

550 g (1 lb 4 oz) corn kernels (fresh,
   canned or frozen)

1 large boiling potato, cut into
   1 cm (½ inch) cubes

185 ml (6 fl oz/¾ cup) cream, plus extra,
   to drizzle

snipped chives, to garnish

1   Melt the butter and oil in a large saucepan over high heat. Cook the chicken in batches for 3 minutes, or until lightly golden and just cooked through. Place in a bowl, cover and refrigerate until needed.

2   Reduce heat to medium and stir in the garlic, leek, celery, bay leaf and thyme. Cook for 2 minutes, or until the leek softens — do not allow the garlic to burn. Add the stock, sherry and 500 ml (17 fl oz/2 cups) water and stir, scraping up any sediment stuck to the bottom of the pan. Add the corn and potato and bring to the boil. Reduce the heat and simmer for 1 hour, skimming any scum off the surface. Cool slightly.

3   Remove the bay leaf and purée the soup. Return to the cleaned pan, add the cream and chicken and stir over medium–low heat for 2–3 minutes, or until heated through — do not boil. Season. Drizzle with extra cream and garnish with chives. If desired, serve with crusty bread.

CHICKEN AND PUMPKIN LAKSA

SERVES 4

2 bird's eye chillies, chopped

2 lemongrass stems, white part only, chopped

4 red Asian shallots, peeled

1 tablespoon chopped ginger

1 teaspoon ground turmeric

3 candlenuts (optional)

110 g (3¾ oz) dried rice noodle sticks

1 tablespoon peanut oil

250 g (9 oz) butternut pumpkin (squash), cut into chunks

800 ml (28 fl oz/3 cups) coconut milk

600 g (1 lb 5 oz) boneless, skinless chicken breasts, cut into cubes

2 tablespoons lime juice

1 tablespoon fish sauce

90 g (3¼ oz/1 cup) bean sprouts

3 tablespoons torn basil

3 tablespoons torn mint

50 g (1¾ oz/½ cup) unsalted peanuts, toasted and chopped

1 lime, cut into quarters

1 **Put paste ingredients** in a food processor with 1 tablespoon of water and blend until smooth.

2 **Soak noodles** in boiling water for 15–20 minutes. Drain.

3 **Heat the oil** in a wok and swirl to coat. Add the paste and stir over low heat for 5 minutes, or until aromatic. Add the pumpkin and coconut milk and simmer for 10 minutes. Add the chicken and simmer for 20 minutes. Stir in the lime juice and fish sauce.

4 **Divide the noodles** among four deep serving bowls, then ladle the soup over them. Top with the bean sprouts, basil, mint, peanuts and lime.

CHICKEN, COCONUT AND GALANGAL SOUP

SERVES 4–6

CHICKEN STOCK

6 red Asian shallots

6 thin slices galangal or ginger

6 coriander (cilantro) roots and stems

500 g (1 lb 2 oz) chicken wings

10 white peppercorns

10 makrut (kaffir lime) leaves, crushed

2 stems lemongrass, bruised

8 thin slices galangal or ginger

1 large red chilli, finely sliced on
    the diagonal

500 ml (17 fl oz/2 cups) coconut milk

2 large boneless, skinless chicken
    breasts, cut into strips

2 tablespoons fish sauce

1 tablespoon lime juice

coriander (cilantro) leaves, to serve

1 **To make** the chicken stock, put all the ingredients and 2.5 litres (87 fl oz/10 cups) of water in a large saucepan and bring to the boil. Reduce the heat and simmer for 1 hour. Strain.

2 **Put the stock,** lime leaves, lemongrass, galangal, chilli and coconut milk in a wok and bring to the boil. Reduce the heat and simmer for 5 minutes. Add the chicken strips and simmer for 5–6 minutes, or until the chicken is cooked. Stir in the fish sauce and lime juice and serve garnished with the coriander leaves.

CHICKEN LAKSA

SERVES 4

CHICKEN BALLS

500 g (1 lb 2 oz) minced (ground) chicken

1 small red chilli, finely chopped

2 garlic cloves, finely chopped

½ small red onion, finely chopped

1 stem lemongrass (white part only), finely chopped

2 tablespoons chopped coriander (cilantro) leaves

200 g (7 oz) dried rice vermicelli

1 tablespoon peanut oil

75 g (2½ oz/¼ cup) good-quality laksa paste

1 litre (35 fl oz/4 cups) chicken stock

500 ml (17 fl oz/2 cups) coconut milk

8 fried tofu puffs, cut in half on the diagonal

90 g (3¼ oz/1 cup) bean sprouts

2 tablespoons shredded Vietnamese mint

3 tablespoons shredded coriander (cilantro) leaves

lime wedges, to serve

fish sauce, to serve (optional)

1 **To make the balls,** process all the ingredients in a food processor until just combined. Roll tablespoons of mixture into balls with wet hands.

2 **Place the vermicelli** in a heatproof bowl, cover with boiling water and soak for 6–7 minutes. Drain well.

3 **Heat the oil** in a large saucepan over medium heat. Add the laksa paste and cook for 1–2 minutes, or until aromatic. Add the stock, reduce the heat and simmer for 10 minutes. Add the coconut milk and the chicken balls and simmer for 5 minutes, or until the balls are cooked through.

4 **Divide the vermicelli,** tofu puffs and bean sprouts among four serving bowls and ladle the soup over the top, dividing the balls evenly. Garnish with the mint and coriander leaves. Serve with the lime wedges and, if desired, fish sauce.

CHICKEN, MUSHROOM AND MADEIRA SOUP

SERVES 4

10 g (¼ oz) dried porcini mushrooms

25 g (1 oz) butter

1 leek (white part only), thinly sliced

250 g (9 oz) pancetta or bacon, chopped

200 g (7 oz) Swiss brown mushrooms, roughly chopped

300 g (10½ oz) large field mushrooms, roughly chopped

2 tablespoons plain (all-purpose) flour

125 ml (4 fl oz/½ cup) Madeira (fortified wine)

1.25 litres (44 fl oz/5 cups) chicken stock

1 tablespoon olive oil

2 boneless, skinless chicken breasts (about 200 g/7 oz each)

80 g (2¾ oz/⅓ cup) light sour cream

2 teaspoons chopped marjoram, plus whole leaves, to garnish

1 **Soak the porcini** in 250 ml (9 fl oz/1 cup) boiling water for 20 minutes.

2 **Melt the butter** in a large saucepan over medium heat and cook the leek and pancetta for 5 minutes, or until the leek is softened. Add all the mushrooms and the porcini soaking liquid and cook for 10 minutes.

3 **Stir in the flour** and cook for 1 minute. Add the Madeira and cook, stirring, for 10 minutes. Stir in the stock, bring to the boil, then reduce heat and simmer for 45 minutes. Cool slightly.

4 **Heat the oil** in a frying pan and cook the chicken breasts for 4–5 minutes each side, or until cooked through. Remove from the pan and thinly slice.

5 **Blend the soup** until smooth. Return to the cleaned saucepan, add the sour cream and chopped marjoram and stir over medium heat for about 1–2 minutes to warm through. Season. Top with the chicken and garnish with marjoram.

CHICKEN AND VEGETABLE SOUP

SERVES 4–6

1.5 kg (3 lb 5 oz) chicken

1 onion

2 large leeks, halved lengthways and well washed

3 large celery stalks

5 black peppercorns

1 bay leaf

2 large carrots, peeled and diced

1 large swede (rutabaga), peeled and diced

2 large tomatoes, peeled, seeded and finely chopped

165 g (5¾ oz/¾ cup) barley

1 tablespoon tomato paste (concentrated purée)

2 tablespoons finely chopped flat-leaf (Italian) parsley

1 Put the chicken, onion, 1 leek, 1 celery stalk, halved, the peppercorns and bay leaf in a large saucepan and add enough water to cover. Bring to the boil, then reduce the heat and simmer for 1½ hours, skimming any impurities that rise to the surface.

2 Strain the stock through a fine sieve and return to the cleaned saucepan. Discard the onion, leek, celery, peppercorns and bay leaf, and set the chicken aside. When it is cool enough to handle, discard the fat and bones, then shred the flesh, cover and chill.

3 Allow the stock to cool, then refrigerate overnight. Skim the fat from the surface, place the stock in a large saucepan and bring to the boil. Dice the remaining leek and celery and add to the soup with the carrot, swede, tomato, barley and tomato paste. Simmer for 45–50 minutes, or until the vegetables are cooked and the barley is tender. Stir in the parsley and shredded chicken. Simmer until warmed through and season.

ASIAN CHICKEN NOODLE SOUP

SERVES 4

3 dried Chinese mushrooms

185 g (6½ oz) thin dry egg noodles

1 tablespoon oil

4 spring onions (scallions), cut into thick matchsticks

1 tablespoon soy sauce

2 tablespoons rice wine, mirin or sherry

1.25 litres (44 fl oz/5 cups) chicken stock

½ small barbecued chicken, shredded

50 g (1¾ oz) sliced ham, cut into strips

90 g (3¼ oz/1 cup) bean sprouts

coriander (cilantro) leaves and thinly sliced red chilli, to garnish

1 **Soak the mushrooms** in boiling water for 10 minutes to soften them. Squeeze dry, then remove the tough stem from the mushrooms and slice them thinly.

2 **Cook the noodles** in a large pan of boiling water for 3 minutes, or according to the manufacturer's directions. Drain and cut the noodles into shorter lengths with scissors.

3 **Heat the oil** in a large heavy-based pan. Add the mushrooms and spring onion. Cook for 1 minute, then add the soy sauce, rice wine and stock. Bring slowly to the boil and cook for 1 minute. Reduce the heat, then add the noodles, shredded chicken, ham and bean sprouts. Heat through for 2 minutes without allowing to boil.

4 **Use tongs** to divide the noodles among four bowls, ladle in the remaining mixture and garnish with coriander leaves and sliced chilli.

SPICY PORTUGUESE CHICKEN SOUP

SERVES 6

2.5 litres (10 cups) chicken stock

1 onion, cut into thin wedges

1 celery stalk, finely chopped

1 teaspoon grated lemon zest

3 tomatoes, peeled, seeded
and chopped

1 sprig mint

1 tablespoon olive oil

2 boneless, skinless chicken breasts

200 g (7 oz/1 cup) long-grain rice

2 tablespoons lemon juice

2 tablespoons shredded mint

1 **Combine the chicken** stock, onion, celery, lemon zest, tomatoes, mint and olive oil in a large saucepan. Slowly bring to the boil, then reduce the heat, add the chicken and simmer gently for 20–25 minutes, or until the chicken is cooked through.

2 **Remove the chicken** from the saucepan and discard the mint sprig. Allow the chicken to cool, then thinly slice.

3 **Meanwhile, add the rice** to the pan and simmer for 25–30 minutes, or until the rice is tender. Return the sliced chicken to the pan, add the lemon juice and stir for about 2 minutes, or until the chicken is warmed through. Season with salt and pepper, and stir through the mint.

CHINESE MUSHROOM AND CHICKEN SOUP

SERVES 4

3 dried Chinese mushrooms

185 g (6 oz) thin dried egg noodles

1 tablespoon oil

4 spring onions, cut into thin strips

1 tablespoon soy sauce

2 tablespoons rice wine, mirin or sherry
(see Note)

1.25 litres (5 cups) chicken stock

½ small barbecued chicken, shredded

50 g (1¾ oz) sliced ham, cut into strips

1 cup (90 g/3 oz) bean sprouts

fresh coriander (cilantro) leaves, to serve

thinly sliced red chilli, to serve

1 **Soak the mushrooms** in boiling water for 10 minutes to soften them. Squeeze dry then remove the tough stem from the mushrooms and slice them thinly.

2 **Cook the noodles** in a large pan of boiling water for 3 minutes, or according to the manufacturer's directions. Drain and cut the noodles into shorter lengths with scissors.

3 **Heat the oil** in a large heavy-based pan. Add the mushrooms and spring onion. Cook for 1 minute, then add the soy sauce, rice wine and stock. Bring slowly to the boil and cook for 1 minute. Reduce the heat then add the noodles, shredded chicken, ham and bean sprouts. Heat through for 2 minutes without allowing the soup to boil.

4 **Use tongs** to divide the noodles among four bowls, ladle in the remaining mixture and garnish with coriander leaves and sliced chilli.

Note: Rice wine and mirin are available at Asian food stores.

CREAMY CHICKEN AND PAPRIKA SOUP

SERVES 4–6

90 g (3¼ oz) butter

1 onion, finely chopped

1 celery stalk, finely chopped

1 small carrot, finely chopped

2 tablespoons Hungarian sweet paprika

40 g (1½ oz/⅓ cup) plain (all-purpose) flour

2 litres (70 fl oz/8 cups) chicken stock

125 ml (4 fl oz/½ cup) cream

300 g (10½ oz) boneless, skinless cooked chicken breasts, finely chopped

crusty bread, to serve

1 In a large saucepan, melt the butter over medium–high heat. Add the onion, celery and carrot and cook for 5 minutes, or until the vegetables have softened.

2 Add the paprika and cook for 1 minute, or until the paprika becomes fragrant. Quickly toss in the flour and stir until well combined. Cook for a further 1 minute and remove from the heat.

3 Add one-third of the stock and mix to a thick paste, stirring out all the lumps. Return the pan to the heat and add the remaining stock. Stir until the soup boils and thickens slightly. Reduce the heat, cover and simmer for 45–50 minutes.

4 Remove the soup from the heat and stir in the cream and chicken. Season to taste and serve with crusty bread.

MAINS

SICHUAN CHICKEN STIR-FRY

500 g (1 lb 2 oz) chicken tenderloins, cut into thin strips

¼ teaspoon five-spice

1 tablespoon Chinese rice wine

1 tablespoon light soy sauce

1 tablespoon chilli bean paste (toban djan)

2 teaspoons Chinese black vinegar

2 teaspoons dark soy sauce

3 tablespoons chicken stock

3 tablespoons peanut oil

1 small red onion, halved and thinly sliced lengthways (not into rings)

2 garlic cloves, crushed

2 teaspoons finely grated fresh ginger

½ teaspoon Sichuan peppercorns, crushed

4 long dried red chillies, cut in half lengthways

1 Put the chicken in a non-metallic bowl and sprinkle the five-spice powder over the top. Add the rice wine and light soy sauce, turn the chicken until well coated, then cover and marinate in the refrigerator for 1 hour.

2 Combine the chilli bean paste, vinegar, dark soy sauce and stock in a small jug.

3 Heat a wok until very hot, add 1 tablespoon of the oil and swirl to coat. Stir-fry the chicken in batches for about 3 minutes, or until browned. Remove each batch and keep warm. Add another tablespoon of the oil, stir-fry the onion for 2 minutes, then remove and set aside with the chicken. Heat the remaining oil in the wok, add the garlic, ginger and peppercorns and stir-fry for 30 seconds, or until fragrant. Add the chilli and stir-fry for 15 seconds, or until it starts to change colour and darken.

4 Return the chicken and onion to the wok, add the sauce and toss for 3 minutes, or until completely cooked through and the sauce has thickened to coat the chicken. Serve immediately with rice.

BALINESE-STYLE NASI GORENG

3 tablespoons vegetable or canola oil

2 eggs, lightly beaten, seasoned with salt and white pepper

150 g (5½ oz/1¼ cups) snake (yard-long) beans, finely chopped

250 ml (9 fl oz/1 cup) vegetable or canola oil, extra, for deep-frying

8 uncooked prawn crackers

3 garlic cloves, chopped

1 onion or 4 red Asian shallots, finely chopped

1 small bird's eye chilli

200 g (7 oz) raw small prawns (shrimp), peeled and deveined

250 g (9 oz) boneless, skinless chicken breasts, thinly sliced

740 g (1 lb 10 oz/4 cups) steamed long-grain rice

4 spring onions (scallions), finely sliced

1 tablespoon kecap manis (Indonesian soy sauce)

1–2 tablespoons light soy sauce

8 iceberg lettuce leaves, trimmed to form a bowl shape

1 tomato, sliced

1 small cucumber, seeded and thinly sliced

1 tablespoon fried red Asian shallots

1 **Heat 1 tablespoon** of oil in a wok over medium heat, add the beaten egg and swirl over the base to create an omelette. Cook over low heat for 3–5 minutes, or until set, then turn out onto a plate and slice thinly. Cook the beans in boiling water for 3 minutes, then drain and refresh under cold water.

2 **In a small saucepan,** heat the extra oil until very hot. Add two prawn crackers at a time and cook for 30 seconds, or until crisp. Drain on crumpled paper towels.

3 **Crush the garlic,** onion and chilli to a rough paste in a mortar and pestle or small food processor. Heat the remaining 2 tablespoons of oil in a wok, swirl to coat, and cook the paste for 1 minute, or until fragrant. Add the prawns and chicken, and stir-fry for 3 minutes, or until the prawns have turned pink. Add 2 tablespoons of water and the beans, and season with salt and freshly ground black pepper. Add the cooked rice, spring onion, kecap manis and soy sauce, stirring continuously until all the ingredients are heated through.

4 **To serve,** put two lettuce leaves on each serving plate and divide the filling among them. Garnish with slices of tomato and cucumber, and top with sliced omelette, broken prawn crackers and fried red Asian shallots.

STEAMED CHICKEN AND FENNEL WITH SALSA VERDE

SERVES 4

1 large fennel bulb (about 500 g/
   1 lb 2 oz), thinly sliced

½ small lemon, thinly sliced

4 boneless, skinless chicken breasts

SALSA VERDE

3 tablespoons finely chopped flat-leaf
   (Italian) parsley

3 tablespoons baby capers

1 large garlic clove, finely chopped

3 tablespoons olive oil

2 teaspoons finely grated lemon zest

2 tablespoons lemon juice

1 **Line a large bamboo** steamer with baking paper and punch with holes. Arrange the slices of fennel and lemon in the steamer and sit the chicken breasts on top. Season with salt and black pepper. Sit the steamer over a wok of simmering water, making sure the bottom of the steamer doesn't touch the water. Steam, covered, for about 15 minutes, or until the chicken is cooked through.

2 **To make salsa verde,** combine all the ingredients in a bowl.

3 **Serve the chicken** with the salsa verde and the slices of fennel.

THREE MUSHROOM GINGER CHICKEN

SERVES 3–4

500 g (1 lb 2 oz) boneless, skinless
chicken breasts, thinly sliced

1 tablespoon Scotch whisky

1 tablespoon light soy sauce

15 g (½ oz) dried black or wood
ear fungus

3 tablespoons peanut oil

2 tablespoons fresh ginger, cut into thin
matchsticks

2 spring onions (scallions), cut into
3 cm (1¼ inch) lengths

1 small red capsicum (pepper),
finely sliced

150 g (5½ oz) fresh shiitake mushrooms,
stems removed, finely sliced

150 g (5½ oz) fresh oyster mushrooms,
finely sliced

1 garlic clove, crushed

3 tablespoons mushroom oyster sauce
or oyster sauce

1 tablespoon mushroom soy sauce

½ teaspoon ground white pepper

1 **Put the chicken** in a non-metallic bowl with the whisky and light soy sauce. Mix to coat, then cover and marinate in the refrigerator for 1 hour. Meanwhile, soak the fungus in boiling water for 20 minutes. Rinse, then finely slice.

2 **Drain the chicken** well. Heat a wok over high heat, add 1 tablespoon of the oil and swirl to coat. Stir-fry the chicken in batches for 2–3 minutes, or until golden brown and tender. Remove and keep warm.

3 **Heat remaining oil,** then add the fungus, ginger, spring onion, capsicum and mushrooms and stir-fry for 1–2 minutes, or until the vegetables are soft. Return the chicken to the wok with the garlic and stir-fry for 1 minute. Add the mushroom oyster sauce, soy sauce and white pepper and stir to combine, cooking for an additional minute until the chicken is cooked through and coated with the sauce.

SWISS-STYLE CHICKEN

4 x 200 g (7 oz) boneless, skinless chicken breasts

1 tablespoon olive oil

40 g (1½ oz) butter

1 garlic clove, crushed

200 g (7 oz/2 cups) button mushrooms, sliced

1 tablespoon chopped tarragon

125 ml (4 fl oz/½ cup) cream

1 tablespoon brandy

4 large slices gruyère or swiss cheese

1   **Heat the grill** (broiler) to high. Place the chicken breasts between two sheets of plastic wrap and pound with a mallet or rolling pin until 1 cm (½ inch) thick. Sit the chicken breasts slightly apart on a lightly oiled grill tray and brush them with the oil. Grill for about 5 minutes, or until cooked through, turning once during cooking. Transfer to a lightly oiled shallow ovenproof dish.

2   **While the chicken** is grilling, melt the butter in a frying pan. Add the garlic and mushrooms and cook over medium heat for 3 minutes, or until the mushrooms have softened. Add the tarragon, cream and brandy and stir over high heat for about 2 minutes, or until the sauce has reduced and thickened.

3   **Spoon hot sauce** over the chicken breasts and top with a slice of cheese. Put the dish under the hot grill and cook for about 4 minutes, or until the cheese has melted. Serve hot.

STEAMED CHICKEN WITH GINGER AND SHALLOT DRESSING

SERVES 4

GINGER AND SHALLOT DRESSING

2 x 2 cm (¾ x ¾ inch) piece fresh ginger, cut into thin matchsticks

125 ml (4 fl oz/½ cup) soy sauce

2 tablespoons Chinese rice wine

1 garlic clove, crushed

½ teaspoon sesame oil

1 tablespoon finely chopped coriander (cilantro) stems

4 spring onions (scallions), thinly sliced on the diagonal

6 kaffir lime leaves, crushed

1 stem lemongrass, (white part only) cut into thirds and bruised

4 x 4 cm (1½ x 1½ inch) piece fresh ginger, sliced

10 g (¼ oz) dried shiitake mushrooms

4 boneless, skinless chicken breasts

700 g (1 lb 9 oz/1 bunch) Chinese broccoli (gai lan), trimmed and cut into thirds

4 tablespoons coriander (cilantro) leaves

1   To make dressing, combine all the ingredients in a bowl.

2   Fill a wok one-third full of water, add the lime leaves, lemongrass, ginger and mushrooms and bring to the boil over high heat. Reduce the heat to a simmer. Line a large bamboo steamer with baking paper and punch with holes. Arrange the chicken breasts on top. Sit the steamer over the wok of simmering water and steam, covered, for 10 minutes, or until the chicken is cooked. Remove and keep warm. Add the Chinese broccoli to the steamer. Steam, covered, for about 3 minutes, or until just wilted. Remove and keep warm.

3   Strain steaming liquid through a sieve, reserving the liquid and the mushrooms. Remove the stems from the mushrooms and discard. Thinly slice the caps and add them to the dressing with 125 ml (4 fl oz/½ cup) of the reserved liquid. Cut each chicken breast into three pieces on the diagonal. Divide the Chinese broccoli among four serving plates. Top with chicken, spoon the dressing over the top and garnish with coriander. Serve immediately.

BARBECUED HONEY CHICKEN WINGS

SERVES 4

12 chicken wings

4 tablespoons soy sauce

3 tablespoons sherry

3 tablespoons oil

1 garlic clove, crushed

3 tablespoons honey

1 **Rinse chicken wings,** then give them a thorough pat with paper towels to dry them. Tuck the wing tips into the underside.

2 **Put chicken wings** in a shallow non-metallic dish. Whisk together the soy sauce, sherry, oil and garlic, then pour over the chicken wings, turning them to coat. Cover with plastic wrap, then leave in the fridge for 2 hours to allow the flavours of the marinade to permeate the chicken — it will help if you turn the wings occasionally.

3 **Warm the honey** long enough for it to become a brushing consistency — either use the microwave or warm it gently in a small saucepan.

4 **Lightly grease** a barbecue or chargrill pan (griddle) and heat it up. Lift the chicken out of the marinade and place in the hot pan. Cook the wings until tender and cooked through, turning occasionally — this should take about 12 minutes. Brush the wings lightly with the warmed honey and cook for a further 2 minutes.

LEMON CHICKEN

SERVES 6

500 g (1 lb 2 oz) skinless chicken breast fillet

1 tablespoon light soy sauce

1 tablespoon Shaoxing rice wine

1 spring onion (scallion), finely chopped

1 tablespoon finely chopped ginger

1 garlic clove, finely chopped

1 egg, lightly beaten

90 g (¾ cup) cornflour (cornstarch)

oil for deep-frying

LEMON SAUCE

2 tablespoons lemon juice

2 teaspoons sugar

½ teaspoon salt

½ teaspoon roasted sesame oil

3 tablespoons chicken stock or water

½ teaspoon cornflour (cornstarch)

1 **Cut the chicken** into slices. Place in a bowl, add the soy sauce, rice wine, spring onion, ginger and garlic, and toss lightly. Marinate in the fridge for at least 1 hour, or overnight.

2 **Add the egg** to the chicken mixture and toss lightly to coat. Drain any excess egg and coat the chicken pieces with the cornflour. The easiest way to do this is to put the chicken and cornflour in a plastic bag and shake it.

3 **Fill a wok** one-quarter full of oil. Heat the oil to 190°C (375°F), or until a piece of bread turns golden brown in 10 seconds when dropped into it Add half the chicken, a piece at a time, and fry, stirring constantly, for about 4 minutes, or until golden brown. Remove with a wire sieve or slotted spoon and drain. Repeat with the remaining chicken.

4 **Reheat the oil** and return all the chicken to the wok. Cook until crisp and golden brown. Drain the chicken. Pour off the oil and wipe out the wok.

5 **To make the lemon sauce,** combine the lemon juice, sugar, salt, sesame oil, stock and cornflour.

6 **Reheat the wok** over medium heat until hot. Add the lemon sauce and stir constantly until the mixture thickens. Add the chicken and toss lightly in the sauce.

CHICKEN MARYLANDS WITH PINE NUT STUFFING

SERVES 4

PINE NUT STUFFING

80 g (2¾ oz/1 cup) fresh breadcrumbs

20 g (¾ oz) butter, melted

2 tablespoons lemon juice

1 teaspoon grated lemon zest

35 g (1¼ oz/¼ cup) currants

40 g (1½ oz/¼ cup) pine nuts

2 teaspoons thyme leaves

4 x 375 g (13 oz) chicken marylands, with skin on

1 garlic clove, halved

½ lemon

375 ml (13 fl oz/1½ cups) chicken stock

1 Preheat a kettle or covered barbecue to medium indirect heat. Meanwhile, put all the pine nut stuffing ingredients in a bowl and combine well.

2 Rub each chicken portion with the cut side of the garlic clove and the lemon. Using your fingers, gently push the stuffing under the skin of each chicken portion, then secure with a small skewer or thick toothpick.

3 Put the chicken in a roasting tin, pour on the stock, then put the tin on the barbecue grill and lower the lid. Roast for 30 minutes, or until the juices run clear when tested with a skewer in the thickest part of the thigh. During cooking, baste the chicken regularly and top up the stock a little at a time as it evaporates to ensure the chicken stays moist. Serve the chicken hot, with roast vegetables and steamed green beans, if desired.

PANANG CHICKEN

SERVES 4

CURRY PASTE

6 long dried red chillies

4 red Asian shallots, roughly chopped

6 garlic cloves, roughly chopped

3 stems lemongrass, (white part only) roughly chopped

6 cm (2½ inch) piece galangal or ginger, roughly chopped

1 teaspoon ground coriander

2 teaspoons ground cumin

6 coriander (cilantro) roots, chopped

2 teaspoons shrimp paste

4 tablespoons toasted peanuts

1 tablespoon vegetable oil

2 tablespoons vegetable oil

2 garlic cloves, crushed

400 ml (14 fl oz) tin coconut milk

1 tablespoon fish sauce

2 teaspoons light brown sugar or palm sugar (jaggery)

600 g (1 lb 5 oz) chicken breast fillets, cut into strips

1 handful coriander (cilantro) leaves

1 long green chilli, seeded and cut into thin strips

1 To make the curry paste, soak the chillies in hot water for 10 minutes. Discard the water and roughly chop the chillies. Place in a small blender with the shallots, garlic, lemongrass, galangal, spices, coriander roots, shrimp paste, peanuts and oil and process to a paste. Alternatively, put all the ingredients in a mortar and pestle, gradually adding each ingredient once the previous one is quite crushed, and grind to a paste. Remove 3 tablespoons of paste and freeze the rest for next time.

2 Heat the oil in a large wok over low–medium heat. Add the garlic and curry paste and stir-fry for 4–5 minutes, or until aromatic. Be careful not to burn the paste or the garlic. Add the coconut milk, increase the heat to medium and simmer for about 5 minutes. Stir in the fish sauce and sugar, then add the chicken and cook, covered, for 10 minutes, or until the chicken is cooked through. Serve on steamed rice, garnished with coriander leaves and strips of green chilli.

Note: This paste recipe makes 3–4 times as much as you need. Put the rest in a ziplock plastic bag and freeze ready for next time. Once the paste is made, this is a really speedy curry.

RED MISO CHICKEN WOK-POT

SERVES 4

2 tablespoons vegetable oil

750 g (1 lb 10 oz) boneless, skinless chicken thighs, trimmed and halved

2 tablespoons fresh ginger cut into thin matchsticks

4 star anise

1 cinnamon stick

1 tablespoon sake

2 tablespoons mirin

2 teaspoons Japanese rice vinegar

125 ml (4 fl oz/½ cup) chicken stock

2 tablespoons Japanese soy sauce

1 tablespoon red miso paste

3 spring onions (scallions), green part only, finely sliced on the diagonal into 3 cm (1¼ inch) slices

1 **Heat a wok** until very hot, add half the oil and swirl to coat. Add the chicken thighs in batches and cook over high heat for 2 minutes on each side, or until browned. Remove from the wok.

2 **Reduce heat** to medium, add extra oil if necessary and stir-fry the ginger, star anise and cinnamon stick for 30 seconds. Add the sake, mirin and vinegar and quickly stir until they evaporate. Pour in the stock, soy sauce and 125 ml (4 fl oz/½ cup) of water, bring to a simmer and cook, stirring, for 2 minutes. Stir in the miso paste, return the chicken to the wok and simmer for about 20 minutes, or until chicken is cooked through and tender. Garnish with the spring onion.

SPICY CHICKEN SCHNITZELS

SERVES 4

4 x 200 g (7 oz) boneless, skinless chicken breasts

1 tablespoon ground coriander

1 tablespoon ground cumin

½ teaspoon chilli powder, or to taste

2 garlic cloves, crushed

2 tablespoons lemon juice

2 tablespoons olive oil

250 g (9 oz/1 cup) thick plain yoghurt

½ teaspoon harissa paste, or to taste

½ teaspoon caster (superfine) sugar

2 tablespoons finely chopped mint leaves, plus extra sprigs, to serve

1 **Place chicken breasts** between two sheets of plastic wrap and flatten them with a mallet or rolling pin until 1.5 cm (½ inch) thick.

2 **In a small bowl,** mix the ground coriander, cumin, chilli powder, garlic, lemon juice and oil together to form a paste. Thoroughly rub the paste all over the chicken fillets, then cover and leave to stand for 10 minutes.

3 **Heat the grill** (broiler) to high. Put the chicken on a lightly oiled grill tray and grill for 6–8 minutes, or until cooked through, turning once.

4 **Meanwhile, blend** 1 tablespoon of the yoghurt in a bowl with the harissa and sugar. Stir in the remaining yoghurt and mint, season to taste and serve with the warm chicken, garnished with extra mint sprigs. This dish is also delicious served cold.

LEBANESE WRAP WITH CHARGRILLED CHICKEN

SERVES 4

3 large boneless, skinless chicken breasts

1 tablespoon olive oil

4 pitta bread rounds

200 g (7 oz) ready-made hummus

200 g (7 oz) ready-made beetroot dip

200 g (7 oz) thick plain yoghurt

3 garlic cloves, crushed

4 tablespoons chopped flat-leaf (Italian) parsley

10 cos (romaine) lettuce leaves, shredded

1 small red onion, thinly sliced

3 roma (plum) tomatoes, thinly sliced

1   Place the chicken breasts between two sheets of plastic wrap and slightly flatten them with a mallet or rolling pin.

2   Preheat a barbecue grill plate, chargrill plate or chargrill pan to medium. Lightly brush the hotplate with oil and grill the chicken for 4 minutes on each side, or until cooked through. Remove from the heat, allow to cool slightly, then slice thinly.

3   Lay the bread rounds on a flat surface and spread evenly with the hummus and the beetroot dip, leaving a 3 cm (1¼ inch) border. Top with the chicken and drizzle with the combined yoghurt and garlic.

4   Sprinkle the parsley, lettuce, onion and tomato lengthways along the centre of each round and roll up tightly, tucking in the ends. Wrap tightly in foil and grill the wraps on the hotplate for 1–2 minutes on each side, or until bread is crisp, pressing down lightly with a spatula during grilling. Unwrap the foil, cut the wraps in half on the diagonal and serve hot.

MARINATED SPATCHCOCK WITH GREEN OLIVE GREMOLATA

SERVES 4

4 spatchcocks (poussins)

125 ml (4 fl oz/½ cup) olive oil

4 garlic cloves, crushed

2 teaspoons finely grated lemon zest

3 tablespoons lemon juice

2 tablespoons finely chopped flat-leaf
(Italian) parsley, plus extra to serve

lemon wedges, to serve

GREEN OLIVE GREMOLATA

100 g (3½ oz) pitted green olives,
finely chopped

2 teaspoons grated lemon zest

2 garlic cloves, finely chopped

1 **Joint the spatchcocks.** Twist each thigh at the thigh joint to separate them from the body. Put the birds breast-side-down on a cutting board and cut along the backbone from the neck to the tail end. Carefully scrape away the flesh on one side of the backbone, cutting into the birds to expose the rib cage. Repeat on the other side of the backbone, being careful not to pierce the breast skin, then remove the ribs and backbones. Scrape away the flesh from each thigh bone and cut away the bone at the joint.

2 **In a small bowl,** combine the oil, garlic, lemon zest, lemon juice and parsley. Put the spatchcock pieces in a shallow non-metallic dish, pour the dressing over and toss well to coat. Cover and refrigerate for 3 hours, or overnight if convenient, turning occasionally.

3 **Nearer to serving time,** make the gremolata. Put the olives, lemon zest and garlic in a small bowl, mix well, then cover and refrigerate until needed.

4 **Heat a barbecue grill** plate, flat plate or chargrill pan to high. Cook the spatchcock for 5 minutes on each side, or until cooked through. Serve at once, with the gremolata, extra parsley and some lemon wedges.

CHICKEN WITH COGNAC AND SHALLOTS

SERVES 4

1 tablespoon olive oil

30 g (1 oz) butter

1.8 kg (4 lb) chicken pieces, trimmed of excess fat

2 tablespoons cognac or brandy

8 French shallots, peeled

2 tablespoons chicken stock

2 tablespoons dry white wine

3 thyme sprigs

1 **Heat the olive oil** and half the butter in a large frying pan over medium–high heat and brown the chicken, in batches if necessary, for 6–8 minutes. Transfer the pieces to a large flameproof casserole dish with a tight-fitting lid. Put the dish over low heat, sprinkle the cognac over the chicken and flame it. To do this, light a match and lower the flame onto the cognac until it ignites, then allow the flame to extinguish itself.

2 **Melt the remaining butter** in the frying pan over medium–low heat and cook the shallots without browning for 5 minutes, or until softened. Add the chicken stock and wine, increase the heat to high and boil, stirring, for 30 seconds to deglaze the pan. Pour the contents of the pan over the chicken and add the thyme.

3 **Cover the casserole** tightly with foil and put the lid on. Cover again with foil if you feel the top isn't completely sealed. Place over very low heat, barely simmering, and cook for 45 minutes, or until tender. Transfer the chicken pieces to a plate and keep warm. Increase the heat under the casserole dish and boil until the juices thicken to a light coating consistency.

4 **Spoon the juices** over the chicken and serve with creamy mashed potato.

CHIANG MAI NOODLES

SERVES 4–6

200 g (7 oz) thin dried egg noodles

1 tablespoon vegetable oil

1 red onion, chopped

2 garlic cloves, finely chopped

2–3 tablespoons red curry paste

1 teaspoon ground turmeric

400 ml (14 fl oz) tin coconut milk

425 g (15 oz) chicken breast fillets, cut into thin strips

2 tablespoons fish sauce

1 tablespoon palm sugar (jaggery)

juice of 1 lime

50 g (1¾ oz) packet fried egg noodles, roughly broken up

2 spring onions (scallions), thinly sliced

1 small handful coriander (cilantro) leaves

crisp fried shallots, to serve (see Note)

1 **Cook the noodles** in a large saucepan of boiling water for 4 minutes. Drain under cold water.

2 **Heat the oil** in a large wok. Add the onion and garlic and stir-fry for 2 minutes, or until lightly browned. Stir in the curry paste and turmeric and stir-fry for 1 minute, or until fragrant. Add the coconut milk and 500 ml (17 fl oz/2 cups) of water. Bring to the boil, then reduce the heat and simmer for about 5 minutes.

3 **Add the chicken strips** and simmer for 5 minutes, or until the chicken is cooked. Stir in the fish sauce, palm sugar and lime juice and simmer for 1–2 minutes, or until the sugar has dissolved.

4 **Divide** the cooked egg noodles among four to six deep bowls and ladle on the chicken and coconut mixture. Top with the fried noodles, spring onion, coriander leaves and crisp fried shallots.

Note: Crisp fried shallots are available in jars at Asian supermarkets.

RED CHICKEN CURRY

SERVES 4

540 ml (18½ fl oz) coconut milk

2 tablespoons red curry paste

5 cm (2 inch) piece fresh ginger, peeled and cut into thin matchsticks

125 ml (4 fl oz/½ cup) chicken stock or water

4 kaffir lime leaves

600 g (1 lb 5 oz) boneless, skinless chicken breasts, cut into thin strips

125 g (4½ oz) green beans, trimmed and cut into 5 cm (2 inch) pieces on the diagonal

2 tablespoons fish sauce

1 tablespoon shaved palm sugar (jaggery) or soft brown sugar

1 tablespoon lime juice

1 large red chilli, thinly sliced on the diagonal

coriander (cilantro) leaves, to serve

1 Heat a wok over medium heat. Add 2 tablespoons of the thick liquid from the top of the coconut milk and the red curry paste and ginger. Cook over low heat for 2 minutes, or until fragrant. Stir in the remaining coconut milk, the stock and lime leaves. Bring to the boil, then reduce the heat and simmer for 10 minutes, or until the mixture is reduced and thickened a little.

2 Add the chicken and green beans. Simmer for 5 minutes, or until the chicken is cooked and the beans are just tender. Stir in the fish sauce, palm sugar and lime juice. Garnish with the chilli and coriander leaves and serve with jasmine rice.

CHICKEN WITH ALMONDS AND ASPARAGUS

SERVES 4

4 tablespoons peanut oil

50 g (1¾ oz/⅓ cup) blanched almonds

2 teaspoons cornflour (cornstarch)

4 tablespoons chicken stock

½ teaspoon sesame oil

2 tablespoons oyster sauce

1 tablespoon soy sauce

3 garlic cloves, crushed

1 teaspoon finely chopped fresh ginger

¼ teaspoon white pepper

1 onion, cut into wedges

500 g (1 lb 2 oz) boneless, skinless
chicken thighs, cut into 3 x 2 cm
(1¼ x ¾ inch) strips

1 carrot, cut into half moons

175 g (6 oz/1 bunch) thin asparagus,
trimmed and cut into 3 cm
(1¼ inch) lengths

60 g (2¼ oz/¼ cup) fresh bamboo
shoots, cut into 1 cm (½ inch) dice

1   Heat **1 tablespoon** of the peanut oil in a wok over high heat, add the almonds and stir-fry until golden. Drain on paper towels.

2   **Combine the cornflour** and stock in a small bowl, then stir in the sesame oil, oyster sauce, soy sauce, garlic, ginger and white pepper.

3   Heat **1 tablespoon** of the peanut oil in the wok over high heat until smoking. Add half the onion and half the chicken strips and stir-fry for 2–3 minutes, or until the chicken is almost cooked through. Remove from the wok. Repeat with another tablespoon of oil and the remaining onion and chicken.

4   **Add remaining peanut oil** to the wok and heat until just smoking. Add the carrot and stir-fry over high heat for 1–2 minutes, or until just starting to brown, then add the asparagus and the bamboo shoots, stir-frying for another minute. Remove the vegetables from the wok and set aside with the chicken.

5   **Stir the cornflour** mixture well, then add to the wok. Stir over medium–high heat until the mixture thickens, then return the chicken and vegetables to the wok, stirring well to combine. Cook for a further 1–2 minutes, or until heated through. Remove to a serving dish and sprinkle with the almonds before serving.

BRAISED CHICKEN WITH VEGETABLES

SERVES 4

3 chicken thighs

3 chicken drumsticks

2 tablespoons vegetable oil

8 baby leeks, white part only, cleaned and cut into 1 cm (½ inch) slices

6 red Asian shallots, quartered

100 g (3½ oz) fresh shiitake mushrooms, thickly sliced

4 tablespoons orange juice

2 tablespoons soy sauce

2 tablespoons dry sherry

2 teaspoons soft brown sugar

2 teaspoons green peppercorns

1 teaspoon sesame oil

2 baby bok choy (pak choy), quartered lengthways

1 **Chop the chicken** thighs and drumsticks into bite-sized pieces through the bone (this is best done with a Chinese cleaver). Heat the oil in a large wok and brown the chicken in batches over high heat for 1–2 minutes. Remove from the wok.

2 **Add the leek** and shallots and stir-fry for 1 minute. Add the mushrooms, stir-fry for 1 minute, then add the orange juice, soy sauce, sherry, sugar, peppercorns and 125 ml (4 fl oz/ ½ cup) of water.

3 **Return the chicken** pieces to the wok. Reduce the heat and simmer, covered, for 20 minutes, or until the chicken is tender. Add the sesame oil and bok choy and cook, stirring, for 1 minute, or until wilted. Serve with steamed rice.

CHICKEN GALANTINE

SERVES 4–6

100 g (3½ oz) minced (ground) chicken
150 g (5½ oz) minced (ground) pork
1 teaspoon green peppercorns
170 ml (5½ fl oz/⅔ cup) Calvados or apple brandy
2 tablespoons pouring cream
½ teaspoon mixed (pumpkin pie) spice
1 egg
50 g (1¾ oz) thickly sliced lean ham, cut into 1 cm (½ inch) dice
35 g (1¼ oz/¼ cup) pistachio kernels
2 kg (4 lb 8 oz) chicken, boned
80 g (2¾ oz) butter, softened

1   Preheat the oven to 170°C (325°F/Gas 3).

2   Put the chicken, pork and peppercorns in a small processor fitted with the metal blade. Whizz in 5-second bursts for 35–45 seconds, or until fine. Add 2 tablespoons of the Calvados or apple brandy, the cream, mixed spice and egg and season with salt and pepper. Whizz in short bursts until just combined. Remove the bowl from the machine and stir in the ham and pistachios.

3   Lay the chicken on a board, skin side down, ensuring that all the flesh is on top of the skin. Season with salt and pepper. Spread the chicken and pork mixture on top, leaving a 3 cm (1¼ inch) border. Roll the chicken into a fat log, tucking in the ends as you roll. Tie the chicken in three or four places with kitchen string to help keep its shape, then secure the seams with short skewers.

4   Rub the butter all over the skin and put the chicken on a wire rack in a roasting tin. Cover the tin with foil, sealing the edges tightly. Bake for 35 minutes.

5   Remove the foil and pour the remaining Calvados or brandy over the chicken. Bake for 50 minutes, basting with the pan juices every 15 minutes. Remove from the oven and set aside to cool, basting once or twice. Wrap the chicken in foil and refrigerate overnight. Cut into thin slices to serve.

DEEP-FRIED QUAIL WITH SPICE SPRINKLE AND DIPPING SAUCE

SERVES 4

2 tablespoons vegetable oil

2 teaspoons light soy sauce

2 teaspoons chilli sauce

2 teaspoons grated palm sugar (jaggery) or soft brown sugar

2 tablespoons chopped coriander (cilantro) roots and stems

3 teaspoons grated fresh ginger

3 garlic cloves, crushed

3 teaspoons red curry paste

8 quail

vegetable oil, for deep-frying

SPRINKLING MIX

2 teaspoons coriander seeds

2 teaspoons white peppercorns

2 teaspoons cumin seeds

pinch of mace

1 cardamom pod

DIPPING SAUCE

3 tablespoons water or coconut milk

1 teaspoon grated palm sugar (jaggery) or soft brown sugar

2 teaspoons lime juice

1 tablespoon fish sauce

1 bird's eye chilli, seeded and thinly sliced

1 **Combine the oil,** soy sauce, chilli sauce, palm sugar, coriander, ginger, garlic and red curry paste in a large shallow bowl. Rub the marinade over both sides of each quail, then put them all in the bowl. Cover and leave to marinate overnight in the refrigerator.

2 **To make the sprinkling mix,** grind the coriander seeds, peppercorns, cumin seeds, mace and cardamom pod in a mortar and pestle or spice mill. Stop grinding while there is still some texture to the mix. Transfer to a small bowl.

3 **To make the dipping sauce,** stir the water and palm sugar together in a small bowl until the sugar dissolves. Add the lime juice, fish sauce and chilli and combine well.

4 **Half-fill a wok** with oil and heat to 170°C (325°F), or until a cube of bread dropped in the oil browns in 20 seconds. Wipe the excess marinade off the quail and add them to the wok a few at a time. Deep-fry each batch for about 4 minutes, or until golden. Drain on crumpled paper towels and serve at once with the sprinkling mix and the dipping sauce.

THAI CHICKEN SAUSAGE ROLLS

SERVES 6–8

500 g (1 lb 2 oz) minced (ground) chicken

1 teaspoon ground cumin

1 teaspoon ground coriander

2 tablespoons sweet chilli sauce

2 tablespoons chopped coriander (cilantro) leaves

80 g (2¾ oz/1 cup) fresh breadcrumbs

2 sheets frozen puff pastry, thawed

1 egg, lightly beaten

1 tablespoon sesame seeds

baby rocket (arugula) leaves, to serve

sweet chilli sauce, extra, for dipping

1 Preheat the oven to 200°C (400°F/Gas 6). Combine the chicken, cumin, coriander, chilli sauce, coriander leaves and breadcrumbs in a bowl.

2 Spread the mixture along one edge of each pastry sheet and roll up to conceal the filling. Place the rolls seam-side down on a tray lined with baking paper, brush lightly with the beaten egg and sprinkle with sesame seeds. Bake for 30 minutes, or until golden and cooked through. Slice the rolls and serve with rocket and sweet chilli sauce.

AROMATIC CHICKEN CURRY

SERVES 4

2 tablespoons Madras curry paste

1 tablespoon soy sauce

1 small red chilli, seeded and chopped

10 cm (4 inch) piece lemongrass

5 cm (2 inch) piece fresh ginger, grated

2 garlic cloves, chopped

2 tablespoons tomato paste
(concentrated purée)

750 g (1 lb 10 oz) boneless, skinless,
chicken thigh, cubed

3 tablespoons vegetable oil

2 red onions, chopped

400 ml (14 fl oz) tin coconut milk

250 g (9 oz/2½ cups) cherry
tomatoes, halved

1 handful Thai or Italian basil leaves

1 **Put the curry paste,** soy sauce, chilli, lemongrass, ginger, garlic, tomato paste and 1 tablespoon of water in a small food processor and blend to a smooth paste. If you don't have a processor, do this either with a mortar and pestle or simply chop everything very finely and combine.

2 **Put the chicken** in a bowl, add the paste and mix it all together, rubbing the paste well into the chicken. Cover and marinate in the refrigerator for at least 30 minutes and up to 12 hours.

3 **Heat** 2 tablespoons of oil in a wok over medium heat. Add the onion and cook for 10 minutes, or until very soft, but not brown. Remove the onion from the wok. Heat the remaining oil in the wok over high heat. Add the chicken and paste in two batches and stir-fry for 5 minutes, taking care not to burn the paste.

4 **Return the onion** and chicken to the wok and add the coconut milk. Bring to the boil, then reduce the heat and simmer, covered, for 20 minutes. Stir in the cherry tomatoes and cook, uncovered, for 5 minutes. Scatter the basil leaves over the top and serve with boiled or steamed rice.

CHICKEN TIKKA WITH GARLIC NAAN AND APPLE RAITA

SERVES 4

100 g (3½ oz/⅓ cup) tikka paste

60 g (2¼ oz/¼ cup) Greek style yoghurt

600 g (1 lb 5 oz) boneless, skinless chicken breast, cut into 3 cm (1¼ inch) cubes

2 small red onions, quartered

oil, for brushing

2 tablespoons chopped coriander (cilantro) leaves

APPLE RAITA

1 green apple, grated

2 teaspoons lemon juice

60 g (¼ cup) sour cream

3 tablespoons chopped mint leaves

GARLIC NAAN

1 garlic clove, crushed

2 tablespoons butter, softened

4 plain naan bread

1 **Stir the tikka paste** and yoghurt together, add the chicken and turn it until it is evenly coated in the tikka mixture. Cover the chicken with plastic wrap and refrigerate it for 4 hours or overnight.

2 **To make the raita,** put the grated apple, lemon juice, sour cream and mint in a small bowl and stir to combine. Cover the bowl and refrigerate it until you are ready to serve.

3 **Mash the crushed garlic** and butter together and brush one side of each piece of naan with about 2 teaspoons of the mixture.

4 **Soak four wooden skewers** in cold water for 1 hour and preheat the barbecue to low–medium direct heat. Thread the chicken and onion pieces onto the skewers and cook them on the flat plate for 5–6 minutes on each side, turning once. A little before the chicken is ready, lightly brush the chargrill plate with some oil. Grill the naan, buttered-side down, for 1–2 minutes, or until the bread is golden and marked. Turn it and grill for another minute on the other side.

5 **Sprinkle the skewers** with the chopped coriander and serve them with the garlic naan and apple raita.

GLAZED SPATCHCOCKS

SERVES 4

4 spatchcocks (poussins), rinsed and
  patted dry with paper towels

1 lemon, cut into wedges

8 garlic cloves, halved

3 tablespoons plum sauce

3 tablespoons oyster sauce

1 tablespoon honey

4 small red chillies, seeded and finely
  chopped

1 **Preheat the oven** to 200°C (400°F/Gas 6). Fill the cavity of each spatchcock with the lemon and garlic, then tie the legs together with string.

2 **Place the spatchcocks** on a rack, then put the rack in a roasting tin and pour in enough water to cover the base of the tin. Cover loosely with foil and bake for 30 minutes. Remove the foil.

3 **Combine the plum sauce,** oyster sauce, honey and chilli and brush over the spatchcocks. Return them to the oven and cook, uncovered, for 40 minutes, or until golden brown and the juices run clear when pierced with a knife. Brush occasionally with the marinade during cooking. Serve with steamed rice and green beans.

CHICKEN AND SEAFOOD JAMBALAYA

SERVES 6

3 tablespoons olive oil

300 g (10½ oz) boneless, skinless chicken thighs, cut into 2 cm (¾ inch) dice

1 onion, finely chopped

2 garlic cloves, finely chopped

1 celery stalk, finely diced

1 red capsicum (pepper), finely diced

1 teaspoon smoked paprika

¼ teaspoon ground white pepper

¼ teaspoon ground black pepper

¼ teaspoon cayenne pepper

½ teaspoon dried thyme

½ teaspoon dried basil

400 g (14 oz/2 cups) long-grain rice

1 litre (35 fl oz/4 cups) chicken stock

400 g (14 oz) tin chopped tomatoes

2 bay leaves

400 g (14 oz) small raw prawns (shrimp), peeled and deveined

200 g (7 oz) squid tubes, cleaned, cut into 4 x 3 cm (1½ x 1¼ inch) pieces and scored

2 tablespoons lemon juice

3 tablespoons chopped parsley

2 spring onions (scallions), green part only, finely sliced

Tabasco sauce, to serve

lemon wedges, to serve

1 Heat the oil in a large frying pan or paella pan over medium–high heat, add the chicken in batches and cook for 2–3 minutes, or until golden. Remove from the pan and set aside. Add the onion, garlic, celery, capsicum, spices and herbs and cook gently for 5 minutes, or until the vegetables are golden.

2 Add the rice to the pan and stir for 1–2 minutes, or until the rice is coated in the spices and appears glossy. Gently stir in the chicken stock, tomatoes and bay leaves, bring to the boil, then reduce the heat to low and cover with a lid or foil. Steam for 15–20 minutes, or until most of the liquid has been absorbed. Arrange the prawns, squid and chicken on top of the rice and replace the lid. Continue steaming over low heat for 10 minutes, or until all the liquid has been absorbed. Leave the jambalaya for 5 minutes, then stir it gently. Pour the lemon juice over the top and garnish with parsley and spring onion. Serve immediately with Tabasco sauce and lemon wedges.

CHICKEN TAMALES

SERVES 4

DOUGH

100 g (3½ oz) butter, softened

1 garlic clove, crushed

1 teaspoon ground cumin

210 g (7½ oz/1½ cups) masa harina
(Mexican flour for tortillas)

4 tablespoons thick cream

4 tablespoons chicken stock

FILLING

1 corn cob

2 tablespoons oil

150 g (5½ oz) boneless, skinless
chicken breast

2 garlic cloves, crushed

1 red chilli, seeded and chopped

1 red onion, chopped

1 red capsicum (pepper), chopped

2 tomatoes, peeled and chopped

sour cream, to serve

chopped coriander (cilantro) leaves,
to serve

1 **To make the dough,** beat the butter with electric beaters until creamy. Add the garlic, cumin and 1 teaspoon of salt and mix well. Add the masa harina and combined cream and stock alternately, beating until combined.

2 **To make the filling,** cook the corn in a saucepan of boiling water for 5–8 minutes, or until tender. Cool, then cut off the kernels with a sharp knife. Heat the oil in a frying pan and cook the chicken for about 5 minutes each side, or until golden. Remove, cool and shred finely. Add the garlic, chilli and onion to the pan and cook for 2–3 minutes, or until soft. Stir in the capsicum and corn and cook for 3 minutes. Add the chicken, tomato and 1 teaspoon of salt and simmer for 15 minutes, or until the liquid has reduced.

3 **Cut 12 pieces** of baking paper into 20 x 15 cm (8 x 6 inch) pieces. Spread a thick layer of dough over each piece, leaving a border at each end. Spoon some filling in the centre, roll up and secure with string. Arrange the parcels in a large steamer in a single layer and cover with a lid. Sit the steamer over a large saucepan or wok of boiling water and steam for 35 minutes, or until firm.

4 **Arrange three tamales** on each plate and serve with sour cream and coriander, and a fresh salad.

CAYENNE CHICKEN PIECES

SERVES 6

500 ml (17 fl oz/2 cups) buttermilk

3 garlic cloves, crushed

1 tablespoon finely chopped thyme

1 teaspoon salt

2 kg (4 lb 8 oz) chicken pieces, skin on (about 12 assorted pieces)

peanut oil, for deep-frying

250 g (9 oz/2 cups) plain (all-purpose) flour

1 tablespoon Hungarian sweet paprika

1½ tablespoons cayenne pepper

1 tablespoon celery salt

2 tablespoons onion powder

lemon wedges, to serve (optional)

1   Combine the buttermilk, garlic, thyme and salt in a large bowl. Add the chicken pieces and stir to coat. Cover tightly with plastic wrap and refrigerate for 24 hours, stirring occasionally.

2   Fill a deep-fryer or large heavy-based saucepan one-third full with peanut oil and heat to 170°C (325°F), or until a cube of bread dropped in the oil browns in 20 seconds. Combine the flour, paprika, cayenne, celery salt and onion powder. Lift the chicken out of the buttermilk but don't shake off the excess. Roll in the flour mixture until thickly coated.

3   Deep-fry the chicken pieces, a few at a time, for about 12 minutes, or until deep golden and just cooked through. Drain well on paper towel and rest in a warm oven while cooking the remaining chicken. Serve with lemon wedges, if desired.

CHICKEN THIGHS WITH PERSIAN SPICE MIX

SERVES 4

8 boneless, skinless chicken thighs, trimmed

grated zest and juice of 2 limes

170 ml (5½ fl oz/⅔ cup) olive oil

1 tablespoon coarse black pepper

2 large handfuls basil leaves, shredded

lime wedges, to serve

PERSIAN SPICE MIX

½ teaspoon cumin seeds

½ teaspoon ground turmeric

1 teaspoon grated lemon zest (see Note)

2 cardamom pods

4 black peppercorns

1 **Place chicken thighs** between two sheets of plastic wrap and gently flatten with a rolling pin. Mix the lime zest, lime juice, oil, pepper and basil in a non-metallic bowl and season with salt. Add the chicken, toss well to coat all over, then cover and marinate in the refrigerator for 2 hours.

2 **Place Persian spice** mix ingredients in a spice grinder with a good pinch of salt and blend to a fine powder. (You could also use a mortar and pestle if you're feeling energetic.)

3 **Heat the grill** (broiler) to medium. Drain the chicken from the marinade and sprinkle with the spice mix. Spread the chicken on the grill tray and grill for 8 minutes on each side, or until cooked through. Serve hot with lime wedges.

Note: For an authentic Persian flavour, instead of the lemon zest, use ½ teaspoon of green mango powder (also called amchoor), if you can find it. Ready-made Persian spice mix is also sold in some speciality food stores.

MOROCCAN-STYLE CHICKEN WITH COUSCOUS SALAD

COUSCOUS SALAD

500 ml (17 fl oz/2 cups) apple juice

370 g (13 oz/2 cups) couscous

½ small red onion, halved and finely sliced lengthways

50 g (1¾ oz/⅓ cup) pistachio nuts, toasted

8 dried apricots, chopped

60 g (2¼ oz/⅓ cup) green olives, pitted and chopped

¼ preserved lemon, pulp removed, rinsed and finely chopped (optional)

1 small handful mint, roughly chopped

1 small handful parsley, roughly chopped

2 tablespoons plain (all-purpose) flour

1 tablespoon ras el hanout (Moroccan spice mix, available at supermarkets)

12 chicken tenderloins, trimmed

2–3 tablespoons olive oil

YOGHURT DRESSING

250 g (9 oz/1 cup) plain yoghurt

2 tablespoons chopped mint

2 teaspoons ras el hanout

1 teaspoon honey

1 Heat the apple juice in a saucepan until hot but not boiling. Put the couscous in a bowl, pour over the apple juice, cover and set aside for 5 minutes. Fluff up with a fork. Toss the remaining salad ingredients through the couscous.

2 Combine the flour and ras el hanout on a flat plate. Coat the chicken tenderloins in the mixture and shake off the excess. Heat the oil in a large non-stick frying pan. Cook the chicken for 2–3 minutes on each side, or until cooked and golden. Add a little more oil, as needed. Slice the chicken.

3 To make yoghurt dressing, combine the ingredients in a bowl. To serve, pile the couscous onto serving plates, top with the chicken slices and spoon over the yoghurt dressing.

CHICKEN BREAST WITH SOY MUSHROOM SAUCE

SERVES 4

2 large dried shiitake mushrooms

4 tablespoons boiling water

2 tablespoons light soy sauce

2 tablespoons Chinese rice wine

½ teaspoon sesame oil

1 tablespoon finely sliced fresh ginger

4 x 200 g (7 oz) boneless, skinless chicken breasts

450 g (1 lb) bok choy (pak choy), ends removed and cut lengthways into quarters

250 ml (9 fl oz/1 cup) chicken stock

1 tablespoon cornflour (cornstarch)

1 Soak the dried mushrooms in the boiling water for 20 minutes. Drain, reserving the soaking liquid. Discard the stalks and finely slice the caps.

2 Combine the soy sauce, rice wine, sesame oil and ginger in a non-metallic dish. Add the chicken and turn it to coat. Cover and marinate in the refrigerator for 1 hour.

3 Line a steamer with baking paper and punch with holes. Place the chicken on top, reserving the marinade, and cover with a lid. Sit the steamer over a wok or saucepan of boiling water and steam for 6 minutes, then turn the chicken over and steam for a further 6 minutes. Place the bok choy on top of the chicken and steam for 2–3 minutes.

4 Meanwhile, put the reserved marinade, mushrooms and the soaking liquid in a small saucepan and bring to the boil. Add enough stock to the cornflour in a small bowl to make a smooth paste. Add the cornflour paste and remaining stock to the pan and stir over medium heat for 2 minutes, or until the sauce thickens.

5 Arrange the chicken breasts and bok choy on serving plates, pour the sauce over the top and serve with steamed rice.

THAI CHICKEN AND MANGO SKEWERS

MAKES 6

LIME AND SWEET CHILLI MARINADE

4 tablespoons lime juice

4 tablespoons fish sauce

3 tablespoons caster (superfine) sugar

3 tablespoons sweet chilli sauce

1½ tablespoons peanut oil

4 tablespoons chopped coriander (cilantro) leaves

1 tablespoon finely chopped lemongrass, white part only

750 g (1 lb 10 oz) boneless, skinless chicken thighs, trimmed and diced into 3 cm (1¼ inch) cubes

2 very firm mangoes, peeled and cut into 3 cm (1¼ inch) cubes

6 lime wedges

1 **Soak six bamboo skewers** in cold water for 30 minutes. Meanwhile, put all the lime and sweet chilli marinade ingredients in a large, shallow non-metallic bowl and mix together well. Add the chicken, toss well to coat all over, then cover and marinate in the refrigerator for 20 minutes, turning once or twice. If you have time, marinate it overnight.

2 **When you're nearly ready to eat,** heat the grill (broiler) to medium. Thread 4 chicken cubes and 3 mango cubes onto each bamboo skewer in an alternating fashion. Place the skewers slightly apart on a lightly greased grill tray and grill for about 8–10 minutes, or until the chicken is golden brown all over and cooked through, turning once during cooking and basting occasionally with the marinade. Serve the skewers hot with the lime wedges.

DEEP-FRIED HONEY CHILLI CHICKEN

SERVES 4

4 boneless, skinless chicken breasts

vegetable oil, for deep-frying

plain (all-purpose) flour, for coating

3 tablespoons honey

2 tablespoons chilli sauce

4 tablespoons lemon juice

2 teaspoons light soy sauce

5 cm (2 inch) piece fresh ginger,
  thinly shredded

4 spring onions (scallions),
  thinly shredded

2 small zucchini (courgettes),
  thinly shredded

1 carrot, thinly shredded

3 spring onions (scallions), extra, sliced
  on the diagonal

1 **Cut each chicken breast** into four pieces. Fill a large wok one-third full of oil and heat to 180°C (350°F), or until a cube of bread dropped in the oil browns in 15 seconds. Coat the chicken pieces lightly with seasoned flour, shaking off any excess. Add a few pieces of chicken at a time to the wok and cook for 3–4 minutes, or until cooked and golden brown. Drain on crumpled paper towels.

2 **Combine the honey,** chilli sauce, lemon juice and soy sauce.

3 **Remove** all but 1 tablespoon of oil from the wok and heat. Stir-fry the ginger, spring onion, zucchini and carrot for about 1 minute. Add the honey and chilli mixture, bring to the boil and cook until a little syrupy.

4 **Return the chicken pieces** to the wok and toss in the sauce and vegetables for 1–2 minutes, or until heated through. Serve on a bed of noodles or rice, garnished with the extra spring onion.

LEMON AND THYME ROASTED CHICKEN WITH ZUCCHINI

SERVES 4

1 x 1.8 kg (4 lb) chicken
12 garlic cloves, unpeeled
10 sprigs lemon thyme
1 lemon, halved
1 tablespoon olive oil
8 small zucchini (courgettes), halved lengthways
2 tablespoons chopped flat-leaf (Italian) parsley
1 tablespoon plain (all-purpose) flour
250 ml (9fl oz/1 cup) chicken stock

1 Remove the giblets and any large fat deposits from inside the chicken, then pat it dry inside and out with paper towels. Season the cavity with salt and pepper and stuff it with unpeeled garlic cloves and the sprigs of thyme. Rub the skin with the cut lemon, making sure that it is evenly coated all over, then brush it with 2 teaspoons of the oil and season with salt and black pepper. Tie the legs together.

2 Preheat a kettle or covered barbecue to medium indirect heat, with a drip tray underneath the grill. Position the chicken on the barbecue directly over the drip tray, close the hood and roast the chicken for 1 hour, or until the juices run clear when it is pierced with a skewer between the thigh and the body.

3 When the chicken has been cooking for about 40 minutes, toss the zucchini with the remaining olive oil and season it with salt and black pepper. Arrange the zucchini on the grill around the chicken, re-cover the kettle and cook the chicken

and the zucchini for 20–25 minutes, or until the zucchini is tender, but not soggy. Put the zucchini in a serving dish and sprinkle it with the parsley. When the chicken is ready, remove it from the barbecue, cover it loosely with foil and leave it to rest for 10 minutes. Remove the garlic from the chicken cavity but do not peel the cloves.

4 If you would like gravy to go with the chicken, pour the contents of the drip tray into a container and skim off as much fat as possible. Tip the remaining juices into a saucepan, add the flour and stir well to combine. Cook the gravy over medium heat for 3–4 minutes, or until it has thickened, then add the chicken stock and any juices that have been released from the chicken while it was resting. Bring the gravy to the boil, then reduce the heat and simmer it for 3–4 minutes. Season the gravy to taste, strain it into a jug and serve with the chicken, garlic and zucchini.

ROAST CHICKEN WITH WASABI

SERVES 4

CHIVE BUTTER

60 g (2¼ oz) butter, softened

2 tablespoons wasabi paste (hot Japanese horseradish paste)

1 garlic clove, crushed

20 g (¾ oz/1 bunch) chives, snipped

2 kg (4 lb 8 oz) whole chicken, rinsed well and patted dry

1 teaspoon vegetable oil

¼ teaspoon sesame oil

¼ lemon

steamed Asian greens and chives, to serve

1 **Preheat the oven** to 200°C (400°F/Gas 6). Put the butter, wasabi, garlic and chives in a small bowl and combine well. Starting at the opening of the chicken, carefully use your fingers to loosen the skin over the whole breast of the chicken. Place the butter under the skin of the chicken and smooth over to evenly distribute.

2 **Combine** the vegetable and sesame oils and smear over the whole chicken. Tie the legs together with string. Squeeze the lemon quarter over the chicken, then sprinkle liberally with sea salt flakes. Place on a rack in a roasting pan and cook for 1 hour 15 minutes, or until the juices run clear when the thickest part of the thigh is pierced with a skewer.

3 **Rest the chicken** for 10 minutes before carving. Drizzle the pan juices each serving. Serve with steamed Asian greens, garnish with chives, and sprinkle with a little more sea salt.

LEMONGRASS CHICKEN AND RICE ROLLS

SERVES 4

4 lemongrass stems, halved lengthways
3 boneless, skinless chicken breasts, halved lengthways
1 tablespoon sesame oil
2 red chillies, seeded and chopped
300 g (10½ oz) Chinese broccoli, halved
300 g (10½ oz) plain rice noodle rolls (see Note)
soy sauce, to serve
lime wedges, to serve

1 **Arrange the lemongrass** in a steamer. Place the chicken on top, brush with the sesame oil and sprinkle with chilli. Cover with a lid. Sit the steamer over a wok or saucepan of boiling water and steam for 5 minutes, or until half cooked.

2 **Place the Chinese broccoli** and rice noodle rolls in another steamer of the same size and sit it on top of the steamer with the chicken. Cover with a lid and steam for a further 5 minutes, or until the chicken is cooked and the broccoli is tender. Cut the chicken into thick slices and serve with the broccoli, noodle rolls, small bowls of soy sauce and wedges of lime.

Note: These rolls are fresh blocks of thin rice noodles rolled into a sausage shape. They are available at Asian food stores.

CHICKEN AND ROCKET SAUSAGES WITH TOMATO SAUCE

MAKES 10

500 g (1 lb 2 oz) minced (ground) chicken

2 spring onions (scallions), finely sliced

2 garlic cloves, finely chopped

50 g (1¾ oz/½ cup) shredded parmesan cheese

40 g (1½ oz/½ cup) fresh breadcrumbs

40 g (1½ oz/1 cup) shredded baby rocket (arugula)

1 egg, lightly beaten

2 tablespoons olive oil

1 small onion, finely chopped

3 garlic cloves, extra, finely chopped

400 g (14 oz) tin chopped tomatoes

2 teaspoons sugar

1 small handful basil, roughly chopped

5 slices of prosciutto, halved

1 Place the chicken, spring onion, chopped garlic, cheese, breadcrumbs, rocket and egg in a bowl and mix thoroughly to combine. With wet hands, form 2 heaped tablespoons of the mixture into a sausage shape. Place on a tray and repeat with the remaining mixture to make 10 sausages. Cover and refrigerate for 1 hour.

2 Meanwhile, heat the oil in a saucepan over low heat and cook the onion and extra garlic for 5 minutes, or until softened. Add the tomatoes, sugar, half the basil and 125 ml (4 fl oz/½ cup) of water and season with salt and freshly ground black pepper. Bring to the boil, then reduce heat and simmer for 15 minutes, or until the sauce has reduced and thickened slightly.

3 Line a steamer with baking paper and punch with holes. Arrange the sausages in a single layer on top and cover with a lid. Sit the steamer over a saucepan or wok of boiling water and steam for 15–20 minutes, or until the sausages are firm and cooked through. Remove the sausages and set aside to cool slightly.

4 Wrap a slice of prosciutto around each sausage, then place under a hot grill (broiler) for 3 minutes each side, or until slightly crisp. Serve with the warm tomato sauce and sprinkle the remaining basil over the top.

CHICKEN AND CORN PIES

MAKES 6

1 tablespoon olive oil

650 g (1 lb 7 oz) boneless, skinless chicken thighs, trimmed and cut into 1 cm (½ inch) pieces

1 tablespoon grated ginger

400 g (14 oz) oyster mushrooms, halved

3 corn cobs, kernels removed

125 ml (½ cup) chicken stock

2 tablespoons kecap manis (Indonesian soy sauce)

2 tablespoons cornflour (cornstarch)

2 large handfuls coriander (cilantro) leaves, chopped

6 sheets ready-rolled shortcrust pastry

milk, to glaze

1 Grease six metal pie tins measuring 9.5 cm (3¾ inches) on the base and 3 cm (1¼ inches) deep. Heat the oil in a large frying pan over high heat and add the chicken. Cook for 5 minutes, or until golden. Add the ginger, mushrooms and corn and cook for 5–6 minutes, or until the chicken is just cooked through. Add the stock and kecap manis.

2 Mix the cornflour with 2 tablespoons water in a small bowl or jug, then stir into the pan. Boil for 2 minutes before adding the coriander. Transfer to a bowl, cool a little, then refrigerate for 2 hours, or until cold.

3 Preheat the oven to moderate 180°C (350°F/Gas 4). Using a saucer to guide you, cut a 15 cm (6 inch) round from each sheet of shortcrust pastry and line the six pie tins. Fill the shells with the cooled filling, then cut out another six rounds large enough to make the lids. Top the pies with the lids, cut away any extra pastry and seal the edges with a fork. Decorate the pies with shapes cut from pastry scraps. Prick a few holes in the top of each pie, brush with a little milk and bake for 35 minutes, or until golden.

CHICKEN AND MUSHROOM RISOTTO

SERVES 4

1.25 litres (44 fl oz/5 cups) vegetable or chicken stock

2 tablespoons olive oil

300 g (10½ oz) boneless, skinless chicken breasts, cut into 1.5 cm (⅝ inch) wide strips

250 g (9 oz) small button mushrooms, halved

pinch of nutmeg

2 garlic cloves, crushed

20 g (¾ oz) butter

1 small onion, finely chopped

385 g (13½ oz/1¾ cups) risotto rice (arborio, vialone nano or carnaroli)

170 ml (5½ fl oz/⅔ cup) dry white wine

3 tablespoons sour cream

50 g (1¾ oz/½ cup) grated parmesan cheese

3 tablespoons finely chopped flat-leaf (Italian) parsley

1 **Bring the stock** to the boil over high heat, reduce the heat and keep at a low simmer.

2 **Heat the oil** in a large saucepan. Cook the chicken pieces over high heat for 3–4 minutes, or until golden brown. Add the mushrooms and cook for 1–2 minutes more, or until starting to brown. Stir in the nutmeg and garlic, season with salt and freshly ground black pepper and cook for 30 seconds. Remove from the pan.

3 **Melt the butter** in the same saucepan and cook the onion over low heat for 5–6 minutes. Add the rice, stir to coat, then stir in the wine. Once the wine is absorbed, stir in a ladleful of the hot stock and cook over moderate heat, stirring continuously. When the stock has been absorbed, stir in another ladleful. Continue like this for about 20 minutes, or until all the stock has been added and the rice is creamy and al dente. (You may not need to use all the stock, or you may need a little extra.) Stir in the mushrooms and the chicken with the last of the stock.

4 **Remove the pan** from the heat and stir in the sour cream, parmesan and parsley. Season before serving.

CHICKEN WITH PONZU SAUCE AND SOMEN NOODLES

SERVES 4

PONZU SAUCE

1 tablespoon lemon juice

1 tablespoon lime juice

1 tablespoon rice vinegar

1 tablespoon tamari (Japanese sweet soy sauce)

1½ tablespoons mirin

2½ tablespoons Japanese soy sauce

5 cm (2 inch) piece kombu (kelp), wiped with a damp cloth

1 tablespoon bonito flakes (bonito is a dried smoked fish)

900 g (2 lb) chicken thighs, trimmed and cut in half across the bone

10 cm (4 inch) piece kombu (kelp)

200 g (7 oz) dried somen noodles

250 g (9 oz) shiitake mushrooms (cut into smaller pieces if too large)

1 carrot, thinly sliced

300 g (10½ oz/6 cups) baby spinach leaves

1 **To make the sauce,** combine all the ingredients in a non-metallic bowl. Cover with plastic wrap and refrigerate overnight, then strain through a fine sieve.

2 **Put the chicken** and kombu in a pan with 875 ml (30 fl oz/3½ cups) water. Bring to a simmer over medium heat and cook for 20 minutes, or until the chicken is cooked, skimming the scum off the surface. Remove the chicken and strain the broth. Transfer the broth and chicken pieces to a 2.5 litre (10 cup) flameproof casserole dish. Cover and cook over low heat for a further 15 minutes.

3 **Meanwhile, cook the noodles** in a large saucepan of boiling water for 2 minutes, or until tender. Drain and rinse under cold running water.

4 **Add the mushrooms** and carrot to the chicken and cook for 5 minutes. Put the noodles on top of the chicken, then top with the spinach. Cover and cook for 2 minutes, or until the spinach has just wilted. Stir in 4–6 tablespoons of the ponzu sauce and serve.

CHICKEN AND PORK PAELLA

SERVES 6

60 ml (2 fl oz/¼ cup) olive oil

1 large red capsicum (pepper), seeded and cut into 5 mm (¼ inch) strips

600 g (1 lb 5 oz) boneless, skinless chicken thighs, cut into 3 cm (1¼ inch) cubes

200 g (7 oz) chorizo sausage, cut into 2 cm (¾ inch) slices

200 g (7 oz) mushrooms, thinly sliced

3 garlic cloves, crushed

1 tablespoon lemon zest

700 g (1 lb 9 oz) tomatoes, roughly chopped

200 g (7 oz) green beans, cut into 3 cm (1¼ inch) lengths

1 tablespoon chopped rosemary

2 tablespoons chopped flat-leaf (Italian) parsley

¼ teaspoon saffron threads dissolved in 60 ml (¼ cup) hot water

440 g (15½ oz/2 cups) short-grain rice

750 ml (26 fl oz/3 cups) hot chicken stock

6 lemon wedges

1 **Heat the oil** in a large deep frying pan or paella pan over medium heat. Add the capsicum and cook for 6 minutes, or until soft. Remove from the pan.

2 **Add the chicken** to the pan and cook for 10 minutes, or until brown on all sides. Remove. Add the sausage to the pan and cook for 5 minutes, or until golden on all sides. Remove.

3 **Add the mushrooms,** garlic and lemon zest and cook over medium heat for 5 minutes. Stir in the tomato and capsicum and cook for a further 5 minutes, or until the tomato is soft.

4 **Add the beans,** rosemary, parsley, saffron mixture, rice, chicken and sausage. Stir briefly and then add the stock. Do not stir at this point. Reduce the heat and simmer for 30 minutes. Remove the pan from the heat, cover and leave to stand for 10 minutes. Serve with lemon wedges.

Note: Paella should have thin crust of crispy rice on the top; this is considered one of the best parts of the dish. For this reason, do not use a non-stick frying pan and do not stir the mixture once the stock has been added. Paellas are traditionally served at the table from the pan.

EASY CHICKEN STIR-FRY

SERVES 4

1 tablespoon cornflour (cornstarch)

2 teaspoons finely chopped ginger

2 garlic cloves, crushed

1 small red chilli, finely chopped

1 teaspoon sesame oil

60 ml (2 fl oz/¼ cup) light soy sauce

500 g (1 lb 2 oz) chicken breast fillet, thinly sliced

1 tablespoon peanut oil

1 onion, halved and thinly sliced

115 g (4 oz/⅔ cup) baby corn, halved on the diagonal

425 g (15 oz) baby bok choy (pak choy), trimmed and quartered lengthwise

2 tablespoons oyster sauce

60 ml (2 fl oz/¼ cup) chicken stock

1 Combine half the cornflour with the ginger, crushed garlic, chilli, sesame oil and 2 tablespoons soy sauce in a large bowl. Add the chicken, toss until well coated and marinate for 10 minutes.

2 Heat a wok over high heat, add the peanut oil and swirl to coat. Stir-fry the onion for 2 minutes, or until soft and golden. Add the chicken in two batches and stir-fry for 5 minutes, or until almost cooked through. Add the baby corn and stir-fry for a further 2 minutes, then add the bok choy and cook for 2 minutes, or until wilted.

3 Mix the remaining soy sauce and cornflour with the oyster sauce and chicken stock in a small bowl, add to the wok and stir-fry for 1–2 minutes, or until the sauce has thickened to coating consistency and the chicken is cooked. Serve immediately with steamed rice or noodles.

GRILLED CHICKEN WITH CAPSICUM COUSCOUS

SERVES 4

200 g (7 oz/1 cup) instant couscous

1 tablespoon olive oil

1 onion, finely chopped

2 zucchini (courgettes), sliced

½ red or yellow chargrilled capsicum (pepper), chopped

12 semi-dried (sun-blushed) tomatoes, chopped

½ tablespoon grated orange zest

250 ml (9 fl oz/1 cup) orange juice

a large handful chopped mint

8 chicken thighs or 4 chicken breasts, skin on

2 tablespoons butter, softened

1 Heat the grill (broiler). Bring 500 ml (17 fl oz/2 cups) water to the boil in a saucepan, throw in the couscous, then take the pan off the heat and leave it to stand for 10 minutes.

2 Heat the oil in a frying pan and fry the onion and zucchini until lightly browned. Add the capsicum and semi-dried tomatoes, then stir in the couscous. Stir in the orange zest, one-third of the orange juice and the mint.

3 Put the chicken in a large shallow baking dish in a single layer and dot it with the butter. Sprinkle with the remaining orange juice and season well with salt and pepper. Grill the chicken for 8 to 10 minutes, turning it over halfway through. The skin should be browned and crisp.

4 Serve the chicken on the couscous with any juices poured over it.

TANDOORI WITH CARDAMOM RICE

SERVES 4

250 g (9 oz/1 cup) plain yoghurt, plus extra for serving

60 g (2¼ oz/¼ cup) tandoori paste

2 tablespoons lemon juice

1 kg (2 lb 4 oz) boneless, skinless chicken breasts, cut into 4 cm (1½ in) cubes

1 tablespoon oil

1 onion, sliced thinly

300 g (10½ oz/1½ cups) long-grain rice

2 cardamom pods, bruised

750 ml (26 fl oz/3 cups) hot chicken stock

400 g (14 oz) English spinach leaves

1 **Soak eight wooden skewers** in water for 30 minutes to prevent them burning during cooking. Combine the yoghurt, tandoori paste and lemon juice in a non-metallic dish. Add the chicken and coat well, then cover and marinate for at least 10 minutes.

2 **Meanwhile, heat the oil** in a saucepan. Add the onion and cook for 3 minutes, then add the rice and cardamom pods. Cook, stirring often, for 3–5 minutes, or until the rice is slightly opaque. Add the hot chicken stock and bring to the boil. Reduce heat to low, cover, and cook the rice, without removing the lid, for 15 minutes.

3 **Heat a barbecue plate** or oven grill (broiler) to very hot. Thread the chicken cubes onto the skewers, leaving the bottom quarter of the skewers empty. Cook on each side for 5 minutes, or until cooked through.

4 **Wash the spinach** and put in a large saucepan with just the water clinging to the leaves. Cook, covered, over medium heat for 1–2 minutes, or until the spinach has wilted. Uncover the rice, fluff up with a fork and serve with the spinach, chicken and extra yoghurt.

CHICKEN CASSEROLE WITH OLIVES AND TOMATOES

SERVES 4

1 tablespoon olive oil

1 large onion, chopped

2 garlic cloves, crushed

8 pieces chicken, skin on

1 tablespoon tomato paste
(concentrated purée)

375 ml (13 fl oz/1½ cups) white wine

a pinch of sugar

8 large ripe tomatoes, chopped

4 tablespoons parsley, chopped

180 g (6½ oz/1½ cups) green beans,
topped, tailed and halved

130 g (4½ oz) olives

1 **Heat the oil** in a large flameproof casserole and fry the onion for a minute or two. Add the garlic and the chicken and fry for as long as it takes to brown the chicken all over.

2 **Add the tomato paste** and white wine, along with the sugar, and stir everything together. Add the tomato and any juices, the parsley and the beans and bring to the boil. Turn down the heat, season well and simmer for 40 minutes.

3 **Add the olives** and simmer for another 5 minutes. The sauce should be thick by now and the chicken fully cooked. Add more salt and pepper, if necessary. Serve with potatoes, pasta or rice.

CHILLI LINGUINE WITH CHERMOULA CHICKEN

SERVES 4

600 g (1 lb 5 oz) boneless, skinless chicken breasts

500 g (1 lb 2 oz) chilli linguine

CHERMOULA

3 large handfuls coriander (cilantro), leaves, chopped

3 large handfuls flat-leaf (Italian) parsley leaves, chopped

4 garlic cloves, crushed

2 teaspoons ground cumin

2 teaspoons ground paprika

125 ml (4 fl oz/½ cup) lemon juice

2 teaspoons lemon zest

100 ml (3½ fl oz) olive oil

1 Heat a large non-stick frying pan over medium heat. Add the chicken breasts and cook until tender. Remove from the pan and leave for 5 minutes before cutting into thin slices. Cook the pasta in a large saucepan of rapidly boiling salted water until al dente, then drain.

2 Meanwhile, combine the chermoula ingredients in a glass bowl and add the chicken. Leave to stand until the pasta has finished cooking. Serve pasta topped with chermoula chicken.

GREEN CHICKEN CURRY

SERVES 4

250 ml (9 fl oz/1 cup) coconut cream

4 tablespoons green curry paste

8 skinless chicken thighs or 4 chicken breasts, cut into pieces

250 ml (9 fl oz/1 cup) coconut milk

4 Thai eggplants or ½ of a purple eggplant (aubergine), cut into chunks

2 tablespoons shaved palm sugar (jaggery) or soft brown sugar

2 tablespoons fish sauce

4 kaffir lime leaves, torn

a handful Thai basil leaves

1–2 large red chillies, sliced

coconut milk or cream, for drizzling

1   Put a wok over a low heat, add the coconut cream and let it come to the boil. Stir it for a while until the oil separates out. Don't let it burn.

2   Add the green curry paste, stir for a minute, then add the chicken. Cook the chicken until it turns opaque. Add the coconut milk and eggplant. Cook for a minute or two until the eggplant is tender. Add the sugar, fish sauce, lime leaves and half of the basil, then mix together.

3   Garnish with the remaining basil, the chilli and a drizzle of coconut milk or cream. Serve with rice.

STIR-FRIED CHICKEN WITH GINGER AND CASHEWS

SERVES 4

1½ tablespoons oil

8 spring onions (scallions), cut into pieces

3 garlic cloves, crushed

8 cm (3 inch) piece ginger, finely shredded

2 skinless chicken breasts, cut into strips

2 red capsicums (peppers), cut into strips

150 g (5½ oz/1½ cups) snow peas (mangetout)

100 g (3½ oz/⅔ cup) cashews

2 tablespoons soy sauce

1½ teaspoons sesame oil

1 Heat the oil in a wok until it is smoking — this will only take a few seconds. Add the spring onion, garlic and ginger and stir them around for a few seconds. Next, add the chicken and stir it around until it has all turned white. Add the red capsicum and keep stirring, then throw in the snow peas and cashews and stir-fry for another minute or so.

2 Once the red capsicum has started to soften a little, add the soy sauce and sesame oil, toss everything together and then tip the stir-fry out into a serving dish.

3 Serve with rice or noodles and more soy sauce, if liked.

THAI CHICKEN WITH GLASS NOODLES

SERVES 4

4 tablespoons coconut cream

1 tablespoon fish sauce

1 tablespoon palm sugar (jaggery) or
   soft brown sugar

2 chicken breasts, skinned and
   cut into shreds

120 g (4½ oz) glass noodles

2 stems lemongrass

4 kaffir lime leaves

1 red onion, finely chopped

a large handful coriander (cilantro)
   leaves, chopped

a large handful mint, chopped

1–2 red chillies, sliced

3 green bird's eye chillies, finely sliced

2 tablespoons roasted peanuts, chopped

1–2 limes, cut in halves or quarters

1 **Mix the coconut cream** in a small saucepan or a wok with the fish sauce and palm sugar and bring to the boil, then add the chicken and simmer until the chicken is cooked through. This should only take a minute if you stir it a couple of times. Leave the chicken to cool in the sauce. Soak the noodles in boiling water for a minute or two — they should turn translucent and soft when they are ready. Drain them, then, using a pair of scissors, cut them into shorter lengths.

2 **Peel the lemongrass** until you reach the first purplish ring, then trim off the root. Make two or three cuts down through the bulb-like root, finely slice across it until it starts to get harder, then throw the hard top piece away. Pull the stems out of the lime leaves by folding the leaves in half, with the shiny side inwards, and pulling down on the stalk. Roll up the leaves tightly, then slice them very finely across.

3 **Put all the ingredients,** except the lime, in a bowl with the noodles and chicken, with its sauce, and toss everything together. Squeeze the lime pieces over the dish and toss again.

HOT AND SWEET CHICKEN

SERVES 4

125 ml (4 fl oz/½ cup) rice vinegar

160 g (5½ oz/⅔ cup) caster (superfine) sugar

6 garlic cloves, crushed

a large pinch of chilli flakes

1 teaspoon ground coriander

1 teaspoon ground white pepper

2 bunches coriander (cilantro), finely chopped, including roots and stems

3 tablespoons olive oil

2 tablespoons lemon juice

8 boneless and skinless chicken thighs, cut in half

2 tablespoons caster (superfine) sugar, extra

2 tablespoons fish sauce

1 small Lebanese (short) cucumber, peeled and sliced

1   Put the vinegar and sugar in a small saucepan, bring to the boil, then turn down the heat and simmer for a minute. Take the mixture off the heat and add two crushed garlic cloves, the chilli flakes and a pinch of salt. Leave to cool.

2   Heat a small frying pan for 1 minute, add the ground coriander and white pepper and stir for 1 minute to make the spices more fragrant. Add the remaining garlic, the fresh coriander and a pinch of salt. Add 2 tablespoons of oil and all the lemon juice. Mix to a paste. Rub over the chicken pieces.

3   Heat the rest of the oil in a wok, add the chicken and fry it on both sides for 8 minutes, or until cooked through. Sprinkle in the extra sugar and the fish sauce and cook for about 2 minutes, or until any excess liquid has evaporated and the chicken pieces are sticky. Serve the chicken with the sliced cucumber and some rice. Dress with the sauce.

BAKED CHICKEN AND LEEK RISOTTO

SERVES 4

60 g (2¼ oz) butter

1 leek, thinly sliced

2 boneless, skinless chicken breasts, cut into small cubes

440 g (15½ oz/2 cups) risotto rice

60 ml (2 fl oz/¼ cup) white wine

1.25 litres (44 fl oz/5 cups) chicken stock

35 g (1¼ oz/⅓ cup) grated Parmesan cheese

2 tablespoons thyme leaves, plus extra to garnish

freshly grated parmesan cheese, extra

1 Preheat the oven to 150°C (300°F/Gas 2) and put a 5-litre (45 fl oz/20 cups) ovenproof dish with a lid in the oven.

2 Heat the butter in a saucepan over medium heat, stir in the leek and cook for about 2 minutes, then add the chicken and stir for 3 minutes. Toss in the rice and stir for 1 minute. Add the wine and stock, and bring to the boil.

3 Pour the mixture into the ovenproof dish and cover. Cook in the oven for 30 minutes, stirring halfway through. Remove from the oven and stir in the cheese and thyme. Season, then sprinkle with extra thyme and cheese.

ROAST CHICKEN PIECES WITH HERBED CHEESE

SERVES 4

150 g (5½ oz) herbed cream cheese
1 teaspoon grated lemon zest
4 whole chicken leg quarters or breasts, skin on
2 leeks, cut into chunks
2 parsnips, cut into chunks
2 teaspoons olive oil

1 Heat the oven to 200°C (400°F/Gas 6). Mix the cream cheese with the lemon zest. Loosen the skin from the whole legs or chicken breasts and spread 2 tablespoons of the cream cheese between the skin and flesh on each. Press the skin back down and season it.

2 Bring a saucepan of water to the boil and cook the leek and parsnip for 4 minutes. Drain them well and put them in a single layer in a baking dish. Drizzle with the oil and season well. Put the chicken on top and put the dish in the oven.

3 Roast the chicken for 40 minutes, by which time the skin should be browned and the cream cheese should have mostly melted out to form a sauce over the vegetables. Check that the vegetables are cooked and tender by prodding them with a knife. If they need a little longer, cover the dish with foil and cook for another 5 minutes. Keep the chicken warm under foil in the meantime.

PULAO WITH FRIED ONIONS AND SPICED CHICKEN

SERVES 4

1 litre (35 fl oz/4 cups) chicken stock

4 tablespoons oil

6 cardamom pods

2 x 5 cm (2 in) piece cinnamon stick

3 cloves

8 black peppercorns

270 g (9½ oz/1⅓ cups) basmati rice

2 handfuls coriander (cilantro) leaves

1 large onion, finely sliced

2 teaspoons curry paste (any type)

1 tablespoon tomato paste
(concentrated purée)

2 tablespoons plain yoghurt

400 g (about 2) skinless boneless,
chicken breasts, cut into strips

plain yoghurt, to serve

mango chutney, to serve

1 Heat the chicken stock in a small saucepan until it is simmering. Heat 1 tablespoon of the oil over a medium heat in a large heavy-based saucepan. Add the cardamom pods, cinnamon stick, cloves and peppercorns and fry for a minute. Reduce the heat to low, add the rice and stir constantly for 1 minute. Add the heated stock and some salt to the rice and quickly bring everything to the boil. Cover the saucepan and simmer the rice over a low heat for 15 minutes. Leave the rice to stand for 10 minutes, then stir in the coriander.

2 Heat 2 tablespoons of the oil in a frying pan and fry the onion until it is very soft. Increase the heat and keep frying until the onion turns dark brown. Drain the onion on paper towels, then add it to the rice.

3 Mix the curry paste, tomato paste and yoghurt together, then mix the paste thoroughly with the chicken strips.

4 Heat the remaining oil in a frying pan. Cook the chicken for about 4 minutes over a high heat until almost black in patches.

5 Serve the rice with the chicken strips, yoghurt and mango chutney.

SAFFRON CHICKEN AND RICE

SERVES 4

60 ml (3 fl oz/¼ cup) olive oil

4 chicken thighs and 6 drumsticks

1 large red onion, finely chopped

1 large green capsicum (pepper) two-thirds diced and one-third cut into thin matchsticks

3 teaspoons sweet paprika

400 g (14 oz) tin chopped tomatoes

250 g (9 oz/1¼ cups) long-grain rice

½ teaspoon ground saffron

1 Heat 2 tablespoons of the oil in a deep frying pan over high heat. Season the chicken pieces well and brown in batches. Remove the chicken from the pan.

2 Reduce the heat to medium and add the remaining oil. Add the onion and diced capsicum, and cook gently for 5 minutes. Stir in the paprika and cook for about 30 seconds. Add the tomato and simmer for 1–3 minutes, or until the mixture thickens.

3 Stir 875 ml (30 fl oz/3½ cups) of boiling water into the pan, then add the rice and saffron. Return the chicken to the pan and stir to combine. Season with salt and pepper. Bring to the boil, cover, reduce the heat to medium–low and simmer for 20 minutes, or until all the liquid has been absorbed and the chicken is tender. Stir in the finely sliced capsicum, then allow it to stand, covered, for 3–4 minutes before serving.

BISTEEYA

SERVES 6-8

250 g (9 oz) butter

1.5 kg (3 lb 5 oz) chicken, quartered

2 large red onions, finely chopped

3 garlic cloves, crushed

1 cinnamon stick

1 teaspoon ground ginger

1½ teaspoons ground cumin

¼ teaspoon cayenne pepper

½ teaspoon ground turmeric

500 ml (17 fl oz/2 cups) chicken stock

a large pinch saffron threads, soaked in 2 tablespoons warm water

1 tablespoon lemon juice

2 large handfuls, chopped flat-leaf (Italian) parsley

2 large handfuls coriander leaves (cilantro), chopped

5 eggs, lightly beaten

100 g (3½ oz/⅔ cup) almonds, roasted, finely chopped

30 g (1 oz/¼ cup) icing (confectioners') sugar, plus extra to serve

1 teaspoon ground cinnamon, plus extra, to serve

12 sheets filo pastry

1 Preheat the oven to 160°C (315°F/Gas 2–3). Melt 150 g (5½ oz) of the butter in a large flameproof casserole over medium heat and brown the chicken well. Set aside. Add the onion and cook until golden. Stir in the garlic and spices, then stir in the stock and saffron water. Add the chicken and turn to coat. Cover and bake, turning occasionally, for 1 hour, or until cooked. Add a little extra water if needed. Discard the cinnamon stick. Drain the chicken, remove the meat from the bones and cut it into small pieces. Increase the oven to 180°C (350°F/Gas 4).

2 Add lemon juice and herbs to the sauce and reduce over high heat for 10 minutes, or until thick. Reduce the heat to very low, gradually stir in the beaten egg, stirring until scrambled, then remove from the heat. Add the chicken meat and season.

3 Mix the almonds with the sugar and cinnamon. Melt the remaining butter. Brush a 1.5 litre (52 fl oz/6 cup) deep pie or baking dish with butter. Put a filo sheet over the dish so the edges overhang; brush with butter. Repeat with 7 more sheets, brushing with butter, slightly overlapping the sheets to give a pinwheel effect. Fill with the chicken mixture. Fold 4 of the filo flaps back over, brush with butter and sprinkle with the almond mixture. Fold the remaining flaps over and tuck the edges into the dish. Brush 4 filo sheets with butter, cut into 15 cm (6 in) squares and scrunch into 'flowers' to cover the pie. Bake for 1 hour, or until golden. Serve sprinkled with the combined extra sugar and cinnamon.

BUTTERFLIED SPATCHCOCK WITH SOFT POLENTA

SERVES 4

4 x 500 g (1 lb 2 oz) spatchcocks (poussins)

4 tablespoons olive oil

1 tablespoon balsamic vinegar

2 tablespoons chopped rosemary leaves

1 tablespoon chopped lemon thyme leaves

1 large lemon, thinly sliced

rosemary sprigs, to serve

thyme sprigs, to serve

POLENTA

1 litre (35 fl oz/4 cups) chicken stock

150 g (5½ oz/1 cup) instant polenta

25 g (1 oz) butter

50 g (1¾ oz/½ cup) finely grated parmesan cheese

1 Cut each spatchcock down each side of the backbone using a large knife or kitchen shears. Discard the backbones, then remove and discard the necks. Turn the spatchcocks over and press down on the breastbone to flatten them out. Remove and discard any excess fat, skin and innards, then rinse well and pat dry with paper towels.

2 Put the oil, vinegar, rosemary, lemon thyme and lemon slices in a large bowl with some freshly ground black pepper. Mix well, add the spatchcocks and turn them about, ensuring the birds are thoroughly coated. Cover with plastic wrap and refrigerate for several hours or overnight.

3 Heat the grill (broiler) to medium. Put the spatchcocks, breast side down, on a large, oiled baking tray and season with sea salt. Grill for 15 minutes, then turn the birds over and grill for a further 15 minutes, or until well browned on both sides and cooked through. Remove from the heat, cover loosely with foil and leave to rest while preparing the polenta.

4 To make the polenta, bring the stock to the boil in a large saucepan. Add the polenta in a thin, steady stream, whisking constantly. Continue whisking over medium heat for about 5 minutes, or until the grains are tender. Remove from the heat, stir through the butter and parmesan and season to taste.

5 Spoon the polenta onto the side of four large serving plates. Sit the spatchcocks on the plates, scatter some rosemary and thyme sprigs over the top and serve.

CHICKEN AND WINTER VEGETABLE PIE

SERVES 6

1 kg (2 lb 4 oz) boneless, skinless chicken thighs, cut into 2 cm (¾ inch) cubes

1 tablespoon plain (all-purpose) flour

4 tablespoons olive oil

1 large leek, finely sliced

2 sticks celery, chopped

2 garlic cloves, crushed

2 carrots, chopped

200 g (7 oz/1½ cups) pumpkin (winter squash), chopped

2 dried mace blades (optional)

500 ml (17 fl oz/2 cups) chicken stock

3 tablespoons thick (double/heavy cream)

3 tablespoons chopped parsley

2 sheets frozen puff pastry, thawed

1 egg, lightly beaten

1 Put the chicken and flour in a large plastic bag and shake until the chicken is coated in flour.

2 Heat half the oil in a large saucepan and cook the chicken over medium heat, in batches, for 5 minutes, or until browned all over.

3 Heat the remaining oil in the same pan, over medium heat, and cook the leek, celery and garlic for 4 minutes, or until the leek is tender. Return the chicken to the pan with the carrots, pumpkin, mace and stock and bring to the boil. Reduce the heat to low and simmer, uncovered, for 30 minutes. Stir in the cream and parsley.

4 Preheat the oven to 180°C (350°F/Gas 4). Cut strips of pastry from one sheet, wide enough to fit the rim of a 23 cm (9 inch) pie dish. Press into place, joining where necessary. Cut two pieces from the remaining pastry and join to the whole sheet, so it is large enough to cover the pie dish.

5 Spoon the chicken mixture into the pie dish and top with puff pastry, pressing into the pastry rim. Trim the edges and press your finger around the edge of the pastry to seal. Using a sharp knife, cut two steam vents in the top of the pie. Brush the pie with a little egg. Bake in the oven for 30 minutes, or until the pastry is golden brown.

ROLLED CHICKEN BREASTS WITH CREAMY LEEKS

4 boneless, skinless chicken breasts

1 tablespoon wholegrain mustard

30 g (1 oz/⅔ cup) baby English spinach

80 g (2¾ oz) shaved ham

60 g (2¼ oz/½ cup) finely chopped semi-dried (sun-blushed) tomatoes

30 g (1 oz) butter

1 leek, white part only, sliced

2 garlic cloves, crushed

170 ml (5½ fl oz/⅔ cup) dry white wine

125 ml (4 fl oz/½ cup) thick (double/ heavy) cream

1 **Lay a chicken breast** between two sheets of plastic wrap on a work surface. Flatten lightly with a meat tenderiser or rolling pin until it is about 1.5 cm (½ inch) thick. Repeat with the remaining chicken breasts. Spread the underside of the breasts with the mustard, top with the spinach and ham and sprinkle with the tomatoes. Roll each up tightly from the thick end, then wrap tightly in a sheet of plastic wrap, twisting the ends to seal well, then wrap again.

2 **Place the rolls** in a steamer and cover with a lid. Sit the steamer over a saucepan or wok of simmering water and cook for 15–20 minutes, or until the chicken feels just firm. Remove the rolls from the steamer and leave for 5 minutes before unwrapping and slicing thickly.

3 **Melt the butter** in a small saucepan over medium heat, add the leek and garlic and cook, stirring, for about 5 minutes, or until softened. Add the wine and simmer until reduced by half. Add the cream, bring just to the boil and stir until the liquid has reduced by half. Spoon the creamy leeks over the chicken.

PERSIAN CHICKEN SKEWERS

SERVES 4

2 teaspoons ground cardamom

½ teaspoon ground turmeric

1 teaspoon ground allspice

4 garlic cloves, crushed

60 ml (2 fl oz/¼ cup) lemon juice

60 ml (2 fl oz/¼ cup) olive oil

4 large boneless, skinless chicken thighs, excess fat removed

lemon wedges, to serve

plain yoghurt, to serve

1 **To make the marinade,** whisk together the cardamom, turmeric, allspice, garlic, lemon juice and oil. Season with salt and ground black pepper.

2 **Cut each chicken** thigh freshly into 3–4 cm (1¼–1½ inch) cubes. Toss the cubes in the spice marinade. Cover thoroughly and refrigerate overnight.

3 **Thread the chicken** onto metal skewers and cook on a hot, lightly oiled barbecue grill or flat plate for 4 minutes on each side, or until the chicken is cooked through. Serve with lemon wedges and plain yoghurt.

CHICKEN WITH MOROCCAN MARINADE

SERVES 4

MARINADE

2 large oranges

2 teaspoons finely chopped fresh ginger

2 garlic cloves

1 teaspoon ground turmeric

1 teaspoon cardamom seeds

½ teaspoon cumin seeds

½ teaspoon paprika

60 ml (2 fl oz/¼ cup) lemon juice

2 tablespoons orange marmalade

½ cup (4 fl oz/125 ml) olive oil

1 large chicken, cut into 8 pieces

12 large green olives

40 g (1½ oz/⅓ cup) toasted slivered almonds

1 **To make the marinade,** zest the oranges, then peel off all the white pith. Remove the segments by cutting between the membranes. Put the orange zest, orange segments, ginger, garlic, turmeric, cardamom seeds, cumin seeds, paprika, lemon juice and marmalade in a small processor fitted with the metal blade. Whizz for 40 seconds, or until combined. With the motor running, pour in the olive oil and whizz for 30 seconds.

2 **Arrange the chicken** in an ovenproof dish or roasting tin, spoon over the marinade and rub it into the chicken with your hands. Cover the dish with plastic wrap and set aside for 30 minutes. Preheat the oven to 190°C (375°F/Gas 5).

3 **Remove plastic wrap** from the baking dish. Sprinkle the olives around the chicken pieces, cover the dish with foil and bake for 25 minutes. Remove the foil, increase the heat to 220°C (425°F/Gas 7) and bake for 12–15 minutes, or until the chicken is golden. Serve sprinkled with the almonds.

PARMESAN-CRUSTED LEMON CHICKEN

SERVES 4

CRUST

3 thick slices day-old white bread, crusts removed

25 g (1 oz/¼ cup) grated parmesan cheese

grated zest of 2 lemons

100 g (3½ oz/1 cup) walnuts

1 tablespoon fresh thyme leaves

1 tablespoon chopped rosemary

1 small handful oregano leaves

sea salt, to taste

60 g (2¼ oz/½ cup) seasoned plain (all-purpose) flour

2 eggs

4 boneless, skinless chicken breasts

lemon wedges, to serve

1 To make the crust, preheat the oven to 150°C (300°F/Gas 2). Cut the bread into chunks, spread on a baking tray and bake for 15–20 minutes, without browning, until completely dry. Cool, then transfer to a small processor fitted with the metal blade. Add the parmesan, lemon zest, walnuts, thyme, rosemary and oregano and whizz for 30 seconds, or until the mixture resembles fine breadcrumbs. Transfer to a large bowl and season with sea salt and freshly ground black pepper.

2 Increase oven heat to 190°C (375°F/Gas 5). Put the seasoned flour in a bowl. Lightly whisk the eggs in another bowl. Coat each chicken breast with the flour, dip into the egg and then coat evenly with the breadcrumb mixture.

3 Put the crumbed chicken breasts on a baking tray lined with baking paper. Bake for 15 minutes, then turn and bake for a further 10 minutes, or until the chicken is cooked through.

4 Slice each chicken piece on the diagonal into four pieces and fan out on serving plates. Serve with lemon wedges.

SPICED QUAIL WITH GRILLED PLUMS

SERVES 4

8 cleaned quail, at room temperature

4 red plums, halved

25 g (1 oz) butter, melted

1½ tablespoons caster (superfine) sugar

½ teaspoon five-spice powder

SPICY MARINADE

3 tablespoons soy sauce

2 tablespoons kecap manis (Indonesian soy sauce)

2 tablespoons Chinese rice wine

2 tablespoons peanut oil

2 teaspoons five-spice powder

3 teaspoons finely grated fresh ginger

1 garlic clove, crushed

1 Using kitchen scissors, cut each quail down both sides of the backbone. Turn the quails over, skin-side-up, and gently flatten the centre of the birds, using the palm of your hand. Using paper towels, clean out the insides. Rinse well and pat dry with paper towels.

2 Put the spicy marinade ingredients in a small bowl and mix together well. Pour into a large shallow dish, add the quail and brush well all over with the marinade. Cover and marinate in the refrigerator for 30 minutes, turning once.

3 Heat the grill (broiler) to high. Put the quail, breast side down, on a large lightly oiled grill tray, shaking off any excess marinade. Grill for 4 minutes, then turn over, baste with the marinade and grill for a further 4 minutes, or until cooked through. Transfer to a warm plate and cover loosely with foil.

4 Put the plums in a shallow tray and brush with the melted butter. Combine the sugar and five-spice powder and sprinkle over the plums. Grill for 3–5 minutes, or until the topping begins to caramelise. Serve the quail with the plums and any juice from the plums. This is delicious served with couscous or a salad of baby Asian greens.

TURMERIC, GINGER AND LIME CHICKEN ON SKEWERS

SERVES 4

8 boneless, skinless chicken thighs

4 limes

MARINADE

250 ml (9 fl oz/1 cup) coconut milk

2 teaspoons ground turmeric

2 tablespoons finely grated fresh ginger

1 tablespoon finely chopped
  lemongrass, white part only

2 garlic cloves, crushed

juice of 1 lime

1 tablespoon fish sauce

2 teaspoons grated palm sugar (jaggery)
  or soft brown sugar

cooked jasmine rice, to serve

1 Cut the chicken into 3 cm (1¼ inch) cubes. Mix all the marinade ingredients in a non-metallic bowl and add the chicken pieces. Cover and refrigerate for 2 hours. Soak 8 bamboo skewers in cold water for 20 minutes.

2 Thread the chicken onto the skewers. Cut the limes in half crossways.

3 Cook skewers on a barbecue flatplate over medium–high heat for 5 minutes, then turn and cook for a further 5 minutes, or until cooked through. Cook the limes, cut-side down, on the flatplate over medium–high heat for 4–5 minutes, or until caramelised.

4 Serve the chicken skewers with jasmine rice, along with the limes for squeezing over the chicken.

MEDITERRANEAN CHICKEN SKEWERS

SERVES 4

2 large boneless, skinless chicken
   breasts, cut into 32 cubes

24 cherry tomatoes

6 cap mushrooms, cut into quarters

2 garlic cloves, crushed

zest of 1 lemon, grated

2 tablespoons lemon juice

2 tablespoons olive oil

1 tablespoon oregano leaves, chopped

1 Soak eight wooden skewers in water to prevent scorching. Thread a piece of chicken onto each skewer, followed by a tomato, then a piece of mushroom. Repeat twice for each skewer and finish with a piece of chicken. Put the skewers in a shallow, non-metallic dish.

2 Combine the garlic, lemon zest, lemon juice, olive oil and chopped oregano, pour over the skewers and toss well. Marinate for at least 2 hours, or overnight if time permits.

3 Cook the skewers on a hot, lightly oiled barbecue grill or flat plate for 4 minutes on each side, basting occasionally, until the chicken is cooked and the tomatoes have shrivelled slightly.

CHINESE STEAMED RICE PARCELS

2 lotus leaves (from Asian supermarkets)

6 dried shiitake mushrooms

275 g (9¾ oz/1¼ cups) short-grain rice

1 tablespoon peanut oil

250 g (9 oz) boneless, skinless chicken thighs, cut into 1.5 cm (⅝ inch) cubes

2 garlic cloves, crushed

3 teaspoons grated fresh ginger

60 g (2¼ oz/⅓ cup) finely diced water chestnuts

1 tablespoon Chinese rice wine

3 tablespoons chicken stock

3 tablespoons light soy sauce

4 spring onions (scallions), thinly sliced

1 teaspoon cornflour (cornstarch)

1 Cut each lotus leaf in half, then soak in hot water for 1 hour. Pat dry with paper towels.

2 Soak the mushrooms in 250 ml (9 fl oz/1 cup) of boiling water for about 20 minutes, then drain, reserving the soaking liquid. Remove the stems and thinly slice the caps.

3 Rinse the rice and put in a saucepan with 375 ml (13 fl oz/1½ cups) of water. Bring to the boil, then reduce the heat to low and cook, covered, for 10 minutes. Remove from the heat and leave, covered, for another 10 minutes.

4 Heat the oil in a wok, add the chicken and cook 3 minutes, or until browned. Add the garlic, ginger, water chestnuts and sliced mushroom and cook for another 30 seconds. Stir in the rice wine, chicken stock, 2 tablespoons of soy sauce, the spring onion and 3 tablespoons of the shiitake soaking liquid.

5 Mix the cornflour with 1 tablespoon of water, add to the wok and cook until the mixture thickens. Stir in the rice and the remaining soy sauce and mix well.

6 Remove the leaves from the water. Put one-quarter of the rice mixture in the centre of each leaf, making a mound about 8 x 6 cm (3¼ x 2½ inches). Fold up the bottom edge, fold in the short sides, then flip the parcel up to completely enclose the filling. Repeat with the remaining mixture and leaves to make four parcels.

7 Put the parcels, seam side down, in a large bamboo steamer. Sit the steamer over a wok of simmering water and steam, covered, for 20 minutes. Serve hot.

CHICKEN WITH MOROCCAN SPICES

SERVES 4

4 boneless, skinless chicken breasts

CHERMOULA

2 garlic cloves, crushed

2 spring onions (scallions), white part only, finely chopped

2 tablespoons chopped coriander (cilantro) leaves

3 tablespoons lemon juice

2 tablespoons olive oil

1 teaspoon ground cumin

1 teaspoon ground coriander

½ teaspoon hot paprika

½ teaspoon chilli powder

COUSCOUS

200 g (7 oz) couscous

4 tablespoons olive oil

4 tablespoons lemon juice

55 g (2 oz/¼ cup) pitted green olives, finely chopped

45 g (1½ oz/½ cup) toasted flaked almonds

85 g (3 oz/⅔ cup) sultanas

4 tablespoons chopped flat-leaf (Italian) parsley

3 tablespoons chopped coriander (cilantro) leaves

1 Cut three slashes across the top of each chicken breast no more than 1 cm (½ inch) deep and put them in a shallow dish. Combine all the chermoula ingredients and pour over the chicken, turning the breasts over to ensure they are evenly coated. Leave to marinate in the refrigerator for at least 1 hour and up to 24 hours.

2 To make the couscous, put 250 ml (9 fl oz/1 cup) of water in a large saucepan with 2 tablespoons of oil and ½ teaspoon of salt. Bring to the boil, then add the couscous. Remove from the heat, cover and leave for about 3 minutes, or until it starts to swell. Return the saucepan to a very low heat for 3 minutes while fluffing up the grains with a fork. Transfer to a bowl and leave to cool for 5 minutes. Stir in the remaining ingredients and season well with salt and pepper.

3 Remove chicken breasts from the chermoula, allowing any excess to drip off. Line a bamboo steamer with baking paper and punch with holes. Arrange the chicken on top in a single layer. Sit the steamer over a wok of simmering water, making sure the bottom of the steamer doesn't touch the water. Steam, covered, for 15 minutes, or until the chicken is cooked through. Serve the chicken with the couscous.

SPICED SPATCHCOCKS WITH WILD RICE STUFFING

SERVES 4

STUFFING

105 g (3½ oz/½ cup) combined wild and
white rice (available at supermarkets)

½ teaspoon salt

40 g (1½ oz) butter

1 stem lemongrass, white part only

½ teaspoon lemon zest

1 tablespoon finely chopped coriander
(cilantro) leaves

1 tablespoon soy sauce

MARINADE

1 teaspoon sichuan pepper, crushed

1 teaspoon coriander seeds, crushed

1 teaspoon sea salt flakes

1 red bird's eye chilli, split in half,
deseeded and finely chopped

1 tablespoon chopped coriander
(cilantro) leaves

1 tablespoon grated fresh ginger

2 garlic cloves, crushed

2 tablespoons soy sauce

1 teaspoon sesame oil

4 x 500 g (1 lb 2 oz) spatchcocks
(poussin)

olive oil, for roasting

roasted pumpkin (winter squash)
and steamed bok choy (pak choy),
to serve

1 To make the stuffing, in a small saucepan bring 185 ml
(6 fl oz/¾ cup) of water, the rice and salt to the boil, stirring
occasionally. Lower the heat, cover and simmer very gently
for 10 minutes. Remove from the heat and allow to stand for
5 minutes. Stir in the butter, lemongrass, zest, coriander and
soy sauce while still warm. Set aside to cool.

2 Put marinade ingredients into a small food processor
and process until smooth. When the stuffing is cool, stuff the
cavities of each of the spatchcocks. Brush the outside of each
with the marinade, cover and refrigerate for 2 hours.

3 Preheat the oven to 190°C (375°F/Gas 5). Place the
spatchcocks onto large roasting trays. Lightly coat with oil
and roast, basting regularly, for 50 minutes to 1 hour, or until
golden and juices run clear when pierced with a sharp knife.
Serve the spatchcocks with roasted pumpkin and steamed
bok choy.

FRAGRANT POACHED CHICKEN WITH SICHUAN SEASONING

SERVES 4

250 ml (9 fl oz/1 cup) light soy sauce
250 ml (9 fl oz/1 cup) Chinese rice wine
150 g (5½ oz/heaped ⅔ cup) sugar
1 large piece (5 cm/2 inch) fresh ginger, unpeeled, sliced
3 garlic cloves, roughly chopped
½ teaspoon ground star anise
2 cinnamon sticks
1 strip orange zest, pith removed
½ teaspoon five-spice powder
½ teaspoon sesame oil
1½ teaspoons sichuan pepper
1.5 kg (3 lb 5 oz) whole chicken, wing tips removed
1 teaspoon vegetable oil
1 tablespoon salt
lemon wedges and steamed bok choy (pak coy), to serve

1 In a large saucepan, combine the soy, rice wine, sugar, ginger, garlic, star anise, cinnamon, orange zest, five spice, sesame oil, and ½ teaspoon of the sichuan pepper. Bring to the boil, add 400 ml (14 fl oz) of water and reduce to a simmer for 15 minutes.

2 Wash the chicken and submerge into the above stock, breast side down. Bring back to the boil and simmer for 30 minutes covered, turning the chicken over for the last 10 minutes. Turn off the heat and let the chicken cool in the stock. Drain the chicken on a wire rack. Preheat the oven to 220°C (425°F/Gas 7).

3 Put remaining sichuan pepper into an ovenproof dish and place in the oven for 5 minutes, or until fragrant.

4 Put the chicken on a roasting tray and brush with vegetable oil. Place in the oven for 20–25 minutes, or until crisp and golden. Crush the sichuan pepper with 1 tablespoon of salt into a fine powder. Slice the lemon into eight wedges.

5 Chop the chicken into pieces and serve with the lemon, sichuan pepper mixture and steamed bok choy.

FIVE-SPICE CHICKEN STIR-FRY WITH CELERY

SERVES 4

3 tablespoons cornflour (cornstarch)

3 teaspoons five-spice, plus
½ teaspoon extra

125 ml (4 fl oz/½ cup) chicken stock

2 tablespoons light soy sauce

1 tablespoon Chinese rice wine
or sherry

2 teaspoons rice vinegar

2 teaspoons caster (superfine) sugar

½ teaspoon sesame oil

500 g (1 lb 2 oz) boneless, skinless
chicken breasts, trimmed and cut
into thin strips

3 tablespoons vegetable oil, for frying

4 spring onions (scallions), white part
chopped, green part reserved

2 stalks celery, cut into 3 cm (1¼ inch)
slices diagonally

1 long red chilli, deseeded and finely
chopped

2 garlic cloves, finely chopped

2 teaspoons grated fresh ginger

steamed jasmine rice, to serve

1 Combine the cornflour and five-spice on a plate. Take 1 teaspoon of the mixture and put in a small bowl with a little stock to form a paste, then add the remaining stock, soy sauce, rice wine, rice vinegar, caster sugar, sesame oil and extra five-spice powder and set aside.

2 Pat the chicken breast strips dry with paper towel and toss in the combined flour and five-spice powder. Shake off any excess. Heat a wok until very hot and add 1 tablespoon of the oil. Stir-fry half the chicken for 3 minutes, or until cooked. Remove to a side plate, add another 1 tablespoon of oil and cook the remaining chicken. Remove to a side plate.

3 Heat remaining tablespoon of oil. Stir-fry the white spring onions, celery, chilli, garlic and ginger for 2–3 minutes, or until aromatic.

4 Return the chicken and combined sauce to the wok. Stir-fry for 2 minutes, or until the sauce has thickened a little and the chicken is hot. Shred the reserved spring onions and use to garnish. Serve immediately with jasmine rice.

GREEN MASALA ON SPATCHCOCK

SERVES 4

MASALA

½ teaspoon fenugreek seeds

3 cloves

5 coriander seeds

5 green cardamom pods, bruised

2 dried bird's eye chillies

3 garlic cloves, crushed

1 teaspoon finely grated fresh ginger

1 handful mint

1 handful coriander (cilantro) leaves

½ small green capsicum (pepper), seeded and chopped

1½ tablespoons cider vinegar

1 teaspoon ground turmeric

1 teaspoon salt

1½ tablespoons vegetable oil

1½ tablespoons sesame oil

4 spatchcocks (poussins)

vegetable oil spray

1 To make the masala, put the fenugreek seeds in a small bowl, cover with water and set aside to soak overnight.

2 Drain the fenugreek seeds and dry on paper towels. Heat a dry heavy-based frying pan over medium–high heat and fry the cloves, coriander seeds and cardamom pods for 2–3 minutes, or until the spices are aromatic. Add the fenugreek seeds and stir for 10–15 seconds. Remove the mixture from the pan and set aside to cool. Transfer to a spice mill and whizz until finely ground.

3 Put the dried chillies, garlic, ginger, mint, coriander, capsicum and vinegar in a mini processor. Whizz in 5-second bursts for 20 seconds, or until puréed. Add the turmeric, salt and ground fenugreek mixture and briefly whizz to combine.

4 Heat the oils in a small frying pan over medium heat. Add the spice paste and fry for 15–20 seconds, or until the oil bubbles. Set aside to cool.

5 Dry the spatchcocks with paper towels. Remove the spines by cutting down both sides of the spine with poultry scissors. Put the spatchcocks on a board, breast side up, and press down firmly with your hand to butterfly them. Rub the masala paste all over the spatchcocks and put them in a shallow non-metallic dish. Cover and chill for 4 hours.

6 Heat the barbecue plate or chargrill pan to medium. Spray lightly with oil and add the spatchcocks, skin side down. Fry for about 10 minutes, or until the skin is crisp and golden. Turn the spatchcocks and fry for 5 minutes, or until cooked through. Serve hot or at room temperature.

BAKED CHICKEN WITH ONIONS AND SUMAC

SERVES 4

2 tablespoons olive oil

1.5 kg (3 lb 5 oz) chicken pieces, skin on, trimmed of fat

5 large onions, cut into thin wedges

3 garlic cloves, chopped

2 tablespoons sumac (see Note)

1½ tablespoons chicken stock or water

Lebanese (large pitta) bread, to serve

green salad, to serve

1   Preheat the oven to 170°C (325°F/Gas 3). Heat half the oil in a large frying pan over medium–high heat. Cook the chicken, in batches, until all the sides are lightly browned. Remove and set aside.

2   Add the remaining olive oil to the frying pan and cook the onions for 10 minutes, or until golden. Add the garlic and sumac and cook for 2 minutes. Spoon half of the onion mixture into a deep baking dish, and arrange the chicken pieces on top. Cover with the remaining onion, pour in the chicken stock and cover with foil.

3   Bake the chicken in the oven for 50–60 minutes. Remove the casserole from the oven and allow to rest for 10 minutes. Season to taste and serve with Lebanese bread and green salad.

Note: Sumac is a purplish-red spice mix with a lemony taste. It is used in Middle Eastern cooking.

CHICKEN WITH HERB PANGRATTATO

SERVES 4

HERB PANGRATTATO

4 slices day-old white bread,
  crusts removed

1 teaspoon dried oregano

2 tablespoons chopped oregano

2 tablespoons chopped basil

2 teaspoons grated lemon zest

½ teaspoon freshly ground black pepper

4 boneless, skinless chicken breasts

4 slices prosciutto

12 sage leaves

plain (all-purpose) flour, for coating

1 egg, lightly beaten

2 tablespoons light olive oil

lemon wedges, to serve

sage leaves, to serve

1 **To make herb pangrattato,** put the bread slices in a small processor fitted with the metal blade. Whizz for 30 seconds, or until breadcrumbs form. Add the dried and fresh oregano, basil, lemon zest and pepper and whizz until well combined.

2 **Slice through** the thick part of each chicken breast, without cutting all the way through, and open out. Cover chicken breasts with plastic wrap and use a meat mallet to gently and evenly flatten them to 1 cm (½ inch) thick. Lay a slice of prosciutto and three sage leaves over each chicken breast. Roll up from the long side; secure with toothpicks.

3 **Put the flour,** egg and herb pangrattato in separate bowls. Coat each chicken roll with the flour, dip into the egg and then roll in the pangrattato. Refrigerate for at least 20 minutes.

4 **Preheat the oven** to 180°C (350°F/Gas 4). Heat the oil in a heavy-based frying pan over medium heat. Add the chicken rolls and fry for 5 minutes on each side, or until golden. Transfer the rolls to a baking tray and bake for 10 minutes, or until the chicken is cooked through. Remove the toothpicks and set chicken aside for 5 minutes before serving. Thickly slice each chicken roll on the diagonal, pile onto plates and serve with lemon wedges and sage leaves.

STEAMED CHICKEN WITH CHINESE VEGETABLES

SERVES 4

5 cm (2 inch) piece fresh ginger,
  finely grated

2 garlic cloves, crushed

1 tablespoon finely chopped coriander
  (cilantro) root

2 tablespoons lime juice

1 teaspoon sesame oil

3 tablespoons soy sauce

500 g (1 lb 2 oz) boneless, skinless
  chicken breast, thinly sliced

100 g (3½ oz) fresh shiitake
  mushrooms, sliced

125 g (4½ oz) other Chinese
  mushrooms (such as enoki, oyster
  or black fungus), torn

125 g (4½ oz) baby corn,
  halved lengthways

coriander (cilantro) leaves, to serve

1 **Combine the ginger,** garlic, coriander root, lime juice, oil and soy sauce in a small bowl.

2 **Put the chicken strips** in a heatproof shallow dish that fits into a large bamboo steamer. Spoon on half the sauce and toss the chicken to coat it in the sauce. Top with mushrooms and baby corn. Put the dish in the steamer basket and pour on the remaining sauce.

3 **Sit the steamer** over a wok of simmering water and steam, covered, for 25 minutes, or until the chicken is cooked through. Garnish with coriander leaves and serve with boiled or steamed rice.

ASIAN-FLAVOURED ROAST CHICKEN

SERVES 4–6

GLAZE

2 tablespoons honey

2 tablespoons soft brown sugar

2 tablespoons soy sauce

½ teaspoon five-spice

1 tablespoon sherry

1 tablespoon chopped fresh ginger

2 garlic cloves, chopped

2 teaspoons sesame oil

1.5 kg (3 lb 5 oz) whole chicken

4 star anise, broken

2 cinnamon sticks, broken

5 cm (2 inch) piece fresh ginger, peeled and chopped

2 garlic cloves, chopped

1 small onion, thickly sliced

1 **Preheat a kettle** or covered barbecue to medium indirect heat.

2 **To prepare glaze,** put all the ingredients in a small saucepan and stir over low heat until the sugar has dissolved. Simmer for 2 minutes, then drain and allow to cool.

3 **Wash the chicken** well with cold water and pat dry with paper towels. Fill the cavity with the star anise, cinnamon sticks, ginger, garlic and onion. Tie the legs together with kitchen string and tuck the wings up underneath the body. Sit the chicken in a lightly oiled disposable foil tray and brush lightly with some of the glaze (reserving the remaining glaze for basting).

4 **Put the tray** on the barbecue, lower the lid and roast the chicken, brushing with the glaze occasionally during cooking, for about 1 hour, or until the juices run clear when tested with a skewer in the thickest part of the thigh. Serve with rice and steamed Asian vegetables such as baby bok choy (pak choy) or choy sum.

CHARGRILLED MUSTARD-MARINATED CHICKEN

SERVES 4

4 boneless, skinless chicken breasts, tenderloins removed

MARINADE

5 cm (2 inch) piece fresh ginger, finely diced

2 garlic cloves, crushed

3 tablespoons dijon mustard

1½ tablespoons soy sauce

1 tablespoon honey

1 tablespoon Chinese rice wine

1 teaspoon sesame oil

2 tablespoons chopped coriander (cilantro) leaves

1 tablespoon vegetable oil

green salad, to serve

1 **Make incisions** diagonally into the chicken with a knife, about 2.5 cm (1 inch) apart.

2 **Combine the marinade ingredients** and rub liberally over the chicken breasts. Place in a bowl and cover. Refrigerate for at least 2 hours.

3 **Heat a barbecue** flat plate or grill plate to medium heat. Brush the flat plate or grill with the oil. Cook the chicken for 7 minutes on each side, or until cooked through and a little charred. Brush the chicken with marinade as it cooks. The chicken is ready when firm to the touch. Serve with a green salad.

SPATCHCOCK WITH MANDARIN BUTTER

SERVES 4

4 spatchcocks (poussin)

125 g (4½ oz) butter, softened

2 garlic cloves, crushed

1 teaspoon mandarin oil, or olive oil mixed with 1 tablespoon orange juice

½ teaspoon tinned green peppercorns, drained and finely chopped

1 **Preheat a kettle** or covered barbecue to indirect medium–low heat. Cut each spatchcock down each side of the backbone using a large knife or kitchen shears. Discard the backbones, then remove and discard the necks. Turn the spatchcocks over and press down on the breastbone to flatten them out. Remove and discard any excess fat, skin and innards, then rinse well and pat dry with paper towels.

2 **In a small bowl,** mix together the butter, garlic, mandarin oil and peppercorns. Push two fingers under the skin of the spatchcock breasts on either side of the central membrane to form two pockets (it doesn't matter if the membrane comes away as well). Gently push a heaped teaspoon of the butter mixture into each pocket. Rub the remaining butter mixture all over each bird.

3 **Sit a rectangular cake rack** on the barbecue plate and rest the spatchcocks on top, skin side up. Lower the lid and roast for about 40–45 minutes, or until the birds are golden brown and the juices run clear when tested with a skewer in the thickest part of the thigh. Alternatively, test the birds using a meat thermometer — they will be cooked when the temperature reaches 85°C (185°F). Serve with baked potato wedges and lightly steamed vegetables

MEXICAN CHICKEN WITH AVOCADO SALSA

SERVES 4

AVOCADO SALSA

1 large avocado, diced

1 large tomato, seeded and diced

½ small red onion, diced

3 tablespoons finely chopped coriander (cilantro) leaves and stems

2 tablespoons extra virgin olive oil

1 tablespoon lime juice

3 teaspoons sweet chilli sauce

1 garlic clove, crushed

4 x 150 g (5½ oz) boneless, skinless chicken breasts

2 x 35 g (1¼ oz) packets taco seasoning

oil, for brushing

CHEESE QUESADILLAS

200 g (7 oz) grated cheddar cheese

1½ tablespoons finely chopped coriander (cilantro) leaves and stems

1 small red chilli, seeded and finely chopped

1 teaspoon sea salt

4 flour tortillas

1 Preheat a barbecue grill plate or chargrill pan to medium. Meanwhile, put all the avocado salsa ingredients in a small bowl, mix well and set aside.

2 Place chicken breasts between two sheets of plastic wrap and flatten slightly with a rolling pin. Put them in a bowl with the taco seasoning and toss well to coat, pressing the mixture in with your hands. Lightly brush the barbecue hotplate with oil, then cook the chicken for about 5 minutes on each side, or until golden and cooked through. Take the chicken off the heat and keep warm. Turn the barbecue up high.

3 To make quesadillas, put the cheese, coriander, chilli and salt in a bowl and mix well. Sprinkle the mixture over one half of each tortilla, then fold the other half over to form a little parcel, pressing the edges together to seal. Brush the grill plate again with oil and cook the quesadillas for about 1 minute on each side, or until grill marks appear. Drain on crumpled paper towels and slice in half.

4 Put a grilled chicken breast on each serving plate with 2 quesadilla halves. Top the chicken with a good dollop of salsa and serve at once.

JAPANESE CHICKEN OMELETTES

SERVES 4

2 x 200 g (7 oz) boneless, skinless chicken breast, trimmed

8 eggs

1 tablespoon soy sauce

1 tablespoon sesame seeds

100 g (3½ oz) snow peas (mangetout), cut into thin matchsticks

1 small daikon, cut into thin matchsticks

1 small carrot, cut into thin matchsticks

100 g (3½ oz/1 cup) snow pea (mangetout) sprouts

SOY AND SESAME DRESSING

1 tablespoon soy sauce

4 tablespoons rice vinegar

2 teaspoons sesame oil

1 **Arrange chicken breasts** in a single layer in a large shallow saucepan. Add enough cold water to cover by about 3 cm (1¼ inches). Bring to a very slow simmer, then cook over low heat for 10 minutes. Turn the heat off and allow the chicken to cool in the cooking liquid.

2 **Whisk soy and sesame** dressing ingredients together in a bowl and season to taste with salt and pepper. Finely shred the cooled chicken breasts and gently toss through the dressing until coated all over.

3 **Heat the grill** (broiler) to medium. Whisk the eggs and soy sauce together in a jug. Put a lightly oiled 26 cm (10½ inch) non-stick frying pan on the stovetop over medium heat. When the pan is hot, pour in a quarter of the egg mixture and swirl it around the base and sides, then quickly remove from the heat and sprinkle with 1 teaspoon of the sesame seeds. Place the pan under the grill for about 1 minute, or until the omelette is lightly browned. Slide the omelette onto a large plate and cover with foil to keep warm. Repeat with the remaining egg mixture and sesame seeds to make four omelettes.

4 **Divide the chicken,** snow peas, daikon and carrot among the omelettes, then fold in the sides to enclose the filling. Serve at once on a bed of snow pea sprouts.

CHICKEN CASSEROLE WITH MUSTARD AND TARRAGON

SERVES 4

60 ml (2 fl oz/¼ cup) olive oil

1 kg (2 lb 4 oz) boneless, skinless chicken thighs, halved, then quartered

1 onion, finely chopped

1 leek, sliced

1 garlic clove, finely chopped

350 g (12 oz/3 cups) button mushrooms, sliced

½ teaspoon dried tarragon

375 ml (13 fl oz/1½ cups) chicken stock

185 ml (6 fl oz/¾ cup) cream

2 teaspoons lemon juice

2 teaspoons dijon mustard

1 Preheat the oven to 180°C (350°F/Gas 4). Heat 1 tablespoon of the oil in a flameproof casserole dish over medium heat, and cook the chicken in two batches for 6–7 minutes each, or until golden. Remove from the dish.

2 Add the remaining oil to the casserole dish and cook the onion, leek and garlic over medium heat for 5 minutes, or until soft. Add the mushrooms and cook for 5–7 minutes, or until they are soft and browned and most of the liquid has evaporated. Add the tarragon, chicken stock, cream, lemon juice and mustard, bring to the boil and cook for 2 minutes. Return the chicken pieces to the dish and season well. Cover.

3 Place the casserole in the oven and cook for 1 hour, or until the sauce has reduced and thickened. Season with salt and pepper and serve with potatoes and a green salad.

CHICKEN WITH CHILLI JAM AND CASHEWS

SERVES 4

CHILLI JAM

10 dried long red chillies

4 tablespoons peanut oil

1 red capsicum (pepper), chopped

1 head (50 g/1¾ oz) garlic, peeled and
roughly chopped

200 g (7 oz) red Asian shallots, chopped

100 g (3½ oz/¾ cup) palm sugar
(jaggery), grated, or soft brown sugar

2 tablespoons tamarind purée
(see Note)

1 tablespoon peanut oil

6 spring onions (scallions), cut into
3 cm (1¼ inch) lengths

500 g (1 lb 2 oz) boneless, skinless
chicken breasts, cut into slices

50 g (1¾ oz/⅓ cup) roasted unsalted
cashews

1 tablespoon fish sauce

15 g (½ oz/½ cup) Thai basil

1 To make chilli jam, soak the chillies in a bowl of boiling water for 15 minutes. Drain, remove the seeds and chop. Put in a food processor, then add the oil, capsicum, garlic and shallots and blend until smooth.

2 Heat a wok over medium heat and add the chilli mixture. Cook, stirring occasionally, for 15 minutes. Add the sugar and tamarind and simmer for 10 minutes, or until it darkens and reaches a jam-like consistency. Remove from the wok.

3 Clean and reheat the wok over high heat, add the oil and swirl to coat. Stir-fry the spring onion for 1 minute, then add the chicken and stir-fry for 3–5 minutes, or until golden brown and tender. Stir in the cashews, fish sauce and 4 tablespoons of the chilli jam. Stir-fry for a further 2 minutes, then stir in the basil and serve.

Note: Tamarind purée is available from Asian supermarkets. Use a non-stick or stainless steel wok because the tamarind will react with the metal in a regular wok and taint the dish.

WILD RICE AND ROAST CHICKEN WITH ASIAN DRESSING

SERVES 8

190 g (6¾ oz/1 cup) wild rice (available at supermarkets)

200 g (1 cup) jasmine rice

1 Chinese barbecue roast chicken (see note)

1 large handful chopped mint

1 large handful chopped coriander

1 large Lebanese (short) cucumber

6 spring onions (scallions)

80 g (2¾ oz/½ cup) roasted peanuts, roughly chopped

80 ml (2½ fl oz/⅓ cup) mirin

2 tablespoons Chinese rice wine

1 tablespoon soy sauce

1 tablespoon lime juice

2 tablespoons sweet chilli sauce, plus extra, to serve

1 **Bring a large saucepan** of water to the boil and add 1 teaspoon of salt and the wild rice. Cook for 30 minutes, add the jasmine rice and cook for a further 10 minutes, or until tender. Drain rice, refresh under cold water and drain again.

2 **Shred the chicken** (the skin as well) into bite-sized pieces, place in a large bowl and add the mint and coriander. Cut the cucumber through the centre (do not peel) and slice thinly on the diagonal. Slice the spring onions on the diagonal. Add the cucumber, spring onion, rice and peanuts to the bowl with the chicken.

3 **Combine the mirin,** rice wine, soy, lime juice and sweet chilli sauce in a small bowl, pour over the salad and toss to combine. Pile the salad onto serving platters and serve with extra chilli sauce.

Note: It is important to use a Chinese barbecued chicken, available from Chinese barbecue shops. The five-spice and soy sauce used to cook it, will add a wonderful flavour to the dish.

BLACKENED CHICKEN WITH CRISPY TORTILLAS

SERVES 4

4 vine-ripened tomatoes, cut into
    1 cm (½ inch) slices

1 teaspoon caster (superfine) sugar

1 red onion, sliced

150 ml (9 fl oz) olive oil

1 ripe avocado

60 g (¼ cup) sour cream

100 ml (3½ fl oz) milk

2 tablespoons lime juice

2 x 16 cm 6¼ inch) corn tortillas

1 teaspoon dried oregano

2½ teaspoons ground cumin

1¼ teaspoons garlic salt

½ teaspoon cayenne pepper

4 small boneless, skinless chicken
    breasts (about 600 g)

1 large handful coriander (cilantro)
    leaves

1 **Place the tomato slices** in a wide dish, sprinkle with sugar and season well. Layer the onion over the top and drizzle with 60 ml (2 fl oz/¼ cup) of oil. Chill for 20 minutes.

2 **Blend the avocado,** sour cream, milk, lime juice and 80 ml (2½ fl oz/⅓ cup) water in a food processor for 1 minute, or until smooth. Season.

3 **Cut each corn** tortilla into eight 2 cm (¾ inch) strips. Combine the oregano, cumin, garlic salt and cayenne pepper, and coat the chicken breasts in the spice mixture, pressing down firmly with your fingers. Heat 1½ tablespoons of oil over medium–high heat in a large, non-stick frying pan until hot. Cook the chicken breasts for 4–5 minutes on each side, or until cooked through. Cool, then refrigerate. In the same pan, add 60 ml (2 fl oz/¼ cup) of oil. Fry the tortilla strips until golden, turning once during cooking.

4 **On each plate** arrange the tomato and onion slices in a small circle. Slice each chicken breast on the diagonal into 2 cm (¾ inch) pieces and arrange over the tomato. Spoon the dressing over the chicken and arrange four tortilla strips over the top. Sprinkle with coriander leaves and serve immediately.

MISO YAKITORI CHICKEN

3 tablespoons yellow or red miso paste

2 tablespoons sugar

60 ml (2 fl oz/¼ cup) sake

2 tablespoons mirin

1 kg (2 lb 4 oz) chicken thighs, boned (skin on)

1 Lebanese (short) cucumber

2 spring onions, (scallions) cut into 2 cm (¾ inch) pieces

1   **Soak 12 long** wooden bamboo skewers in cold water for at least 10 minutes. Place the miso, sugar, sake and mirin in a small saucepan over medium heat and cook, stirring well, for 2 minutes, or until the sauce is smooth and the sugar has dissolved completely.

2   **Cut the chicken** into 2.5 cm (1 inch) cubes. Seed the cucumber and cut into 2 cm (¾ inch) matchsticks. Thread the chicken, cucumber and spring onion pieces alternately onto the skewers — you should have three pieces of chicken, three pieces of cucumber and three pieces of spring onion per skewer.

3   **Cook on a chargrill** plate over high heat, turning occasionally, for 10 minutes, or until the chicken is almost cooked. Brush with the miso sauce and continue cooking, then turn and brush the other side. Repeat this process once or twice until the chicken and vegetables are cooked. Serve immediately with rice and salad.

CHARGRILLED CHICKEN WITH SPINACH AND RASPBERRIES

SERVES 4

60 ml (2 fl oz/¼ cup) raspberry vinegar

2 tablespoons lime juice

2 garlic cloves, crushed

2 tablespoons chopped oregano

1 teaspoon soft brown sugar

2 small red chillies, finely chopped

125 ml (4 fl oz/½ cup) virgin olive oil

4 boneless, skinless chicken breasts

1 teaspoon dijon mustard

200 g (7 oz/ 2 cups) baby English spinach leaves

250 g (9 oz/1½ cups) fresh raspberries

1 Mix 2 tablespoons of the raspberry vinegar, the lime juice, crushed garlic, 1 tablespoon of the oregano, the sugar, chilli and 60 ml (¼ cup) of the oil in a large bowl. Immerse the chicken in the marinade, cover and refrigerate for 2 hours.

2 Preheat the oven to 180°C (350°F/ Gas 4). Heat a chargrill pan and cook the chicken for 3 minutes on each side, then place on a baking tray and bake for a further 5 minutes, or until cooked through. Allow the chicken to rest for 5 minutes, then cut each breast into five strips on the diagonal.

3 To make dressing, combine the remaining oil, vinegar and oregano with the mustard, ¼ teaspoon salt and freshly ground black pepper and mix well. Toss the spinach and raspberries with half of the dressing. Top with the chicken and drizzle with the remaining dressing.

CHICKEN AND TZATZIKI WRAP

SERVES 4

½ telegraph (long) cucumber, seeded and grated

100 g (3½ oz/½ cup) low-fat plain yoghurt

¼ teaspoon lemon juice

1 tablespoon chopped mint

4 boneless, skinless chicken thighs

pinch paprika

4 sheets lavash or other flat bread (see Note)

4 large butter lettuce leaves

1 Sprinkle the grated cucumber with ½ teaspoon salt. Leave the cucumber for 10 minutes, then drain and mix with the yoghurt, lemon juice and mint. Season.

2 Flatten the chicken thighs with a meat mallet or rolling pin, season and sprinkle with the paprika. Grill (broil) the chicken for 5–7 minutes on each side, or until cooked through.

3 Lay out the unleavened breads and place a large butter lettuce leaf on each. Spread each with one quarter of the tzatziki, then top with a sliced chicken thigh. Roll up, folding one end closed. Wrap in baking paper to serve.

Note: If you can't find lavash, use any thin, flat bread that will roll up easily.

BUTTER CHICKEN

SERVES 4–6

2 tablespoons peanut oil
1 kg (2 lb 4 oz) boneless, skinless chicken thighs, quartered
100 g (3½ oz) butter or ghee
3 teaspoons garam masala
2 teaspoons sweet paprika
1 tablespoon ground coriander
1 tablespoon finely chopped ginger
3 teaspoons ground cumin
2 garlic cloves, crushed
¼ teaspoon chilli powder
1 cinnamon stick
5 cardamom pods, bruised
2½ tablespoons tomato paste (concentrated purée)
1 tablespoon sugar
90 g (3¼ oz/⅓ cup) plain yoghurt
185 ml (6 fl oz/¾ cup) cream
1 tablespoon lemon juice

1 Heat a frying pan or wok until very hot, add 1 tablespoon oil and swirl to coat. Add half the chicken thighs and stir-fry for 4 minutes, or until browned. Remove from the pan. Add extra oil, as needed, and cook the remaining chicken. Remove from pan and set aside.

2 Reduce the heat, add the butter to the pan or wok and melt. Add the garam masala, sweet paprika, coriander, ginger, cumin, garlic, chilli powder, cinnamon stick and cardamom pods, and stir-fry for 1 minute, or until fragrant. Return the chicken to the pan and mix in the spices so it is well coated.

3 Add the tomato paste and sugar, and simmer, stirring, for 15 minutes, or until the chicken is tender and the sauce has thickened. Add the yoghurt, cream and lemon juice and simmer for 5 minutes, or until the sauce has thickened slightly. Serve with steamed rice.

CHICKEN CURRY WITH APRICOTS

SERVES 6–8

1 tablespoon ghee or oil

2 x 1.5 kg (3 lb 5 oz) chickens, jointed

3 onions, finely sliced

1 teaspoon grated ginger

3 garlic cloves, crushed

3 long green chillies, seeded and finely chopped

1 teaspoon cumin seeds

1 teaspoon chilli powder

½ teaspoon ground turmeric

4 cardamom pods, bruised

4 large tomatoes, peeled and cut into eight pieces

18 dried 'ready-to-eat' apricots

1   Melt the ghee or add the oil to a large saucepan, add the chicken in batches and cook over high heat for 4–5 minutes, or until browned. Remove from the pan. Add the onion, ginger, garlic and chopped green chilli, and cook, stirring often, for 5 minutes, or until the onion has softened and turned golden brown. Stir in the cumin seeds, chilli powder and ground turmeric, and cook for a further 1 minute.

2   Return the chicken to the pan, add the cardamom, tomato and apricots, with any remaining liquid, and mix well. Simmer, covered, for 30 minutes, or until the chicken is tender and cooked through.

RICH CHICKEN KOFTAS

SERVES 4

KOFTAS

2 tablespoons oil

1 onion, finely chopped

1 garlic clove, crushed

1 teaspoon finely chopped ginger

1 teaspoon ground cumin

1 teaspoon garam masala

½ teaspoon ground turmeric

650 g (1 lb 7 oz) boneless, skinless chicken thighs, trimmed

2 tablespoons chopped coriander (cilantro) leaves

1 onion, roughly chopped

1 tablespoon ghee or oil

2 garlic cloves, crushed

2 teaspoons garam masala

½ teaspoon ground turmeric

170 ml (5½ fl oz/⅔ cup) coconut milk

90 g (3¼ oz/⅓ cup) plain yoghurt

125 ml (4 fl oz/½ cup) cream

35 g (1¼ oz/⅓ cup) ground almonds

2 tablespoons chopped coriander (cilantro) leaves

1 To make the koftas, heat half the oil in a frying pan. Add the onion, garlic, ginger, ground cumin, garam masala and ground turmeric, and cook, stirring, for 4–6 minutes, or until the onion is tender and spices are fragrant. Allow to cool.

2 Place the chicken thighs in batches in a food processor and process until just chopped. Do not over-process. Put the chicken, onion mixture, coriander and ½ teaspoon salt in a bowl and combine well. Using wetted hands, measure 1 tablespoon of mixture and shape into a ball. Repeat with the remaining mixture.

3 Heat the remaining oil in a heavy-based frying pan. Add koftas in batches and cook for 5 minutes, or until well browned all over. Remove from the pan and cover. Put the onion in a food processor and process until smooth.

4 Heat the ghee or oil in a frying pan. Add the onion and garlic, and cook, stirring, for 5 minutes, or until the onion juices evaporate and the mixture starts to thicken. Add the garam masala and turmeric, and cook for a further 2 minutes. Add the coconut milk, yoghurt, cream and ground almonds. Gently bring almost to the boil, then reduce the heat to medium and add the koftas. Cook, stirring occasionally, for 15 minutes, or until the koftas are cooked through. Stir in the coriander and serve.

THAI GREEN CHICKEN CURRY

SERVES 4–6

GREEN CURRY PASTE

1 teaspoon white peppercorns

2 tablespoons coriander seeds

1 teaspoon cumin seeds

2 teaspoons shrimp paste

1 teaspoon sea salt

4 lemongrass stems, white part only, finely sliced

2 teaspoons chopped galangal

1 kaffir lime leaf, finely shredded

1 tablespoon chopped coriander (cilantro) root

5 red Asian shallots, chopped

10 garlic cloves, crushed

16 long green chillies, seeded, chopped

500 ml (17 fl oz/2 cups) coconut cream (do not shake the tins)

2 tablespoons shaved palm sugar (jaggery) or soft brown sugar

2 tablespoons fish sauce

4 kaffir lime leaves, finely shredded

1 kg (2 lb 4 oz) boneless, skinless chicken thigh or breast, cut into thick strips

200 g (7 oz/1 cup) bamboo shoots, cut into thick strips

100 g (3½ oz/1 cup) snake (yard-long) beans, cut into 5 cm (2 inch) lengths

1 handful Thai basil

1 **Dry-fry the peppercorns,** coriander seeds, cumin seeds and shrimp paste wrapped in foil in a frying pan over medium–high heat for 2–3 minutes, or until fragrant. Allow to cool. Using a mortar with a pestle, or a spice grinder, crush or grind the peppercorns, coriander and cumin to a powder.

2 **Put the shrimp paste** and ground spices with the remaining curry paste ingredients in a food processor, or in a mortar with a pestle, and process or pound to a smooth paste.

3 **Put the thick** coconut cream from the top of the tins in a saucepan, bring to a rapid simmer over medium heat, stirring occasionally, and cook for about 8 minutes, or until the mixture 'splits' (the oil starts to separate). Add 4 tablespoons of the made green curry paste, then simmer for 10 minutes, or until fragrant. Add the palm sugar, fish sauce and lime leaves to the pan.

4 **Stir** in the remaining coconut cream and the chicken, bamboo shoots and beans, and simmer for 15 minutes, or until the chicken is tender. Stir in the Thai basil and serve.

BACON-WRAPPED CHICKEN

SERVES 6

2 tablespoons olive oil	
2 tablespoons lime juice	
¼ teaspoon ground coriander	
6 boneless, skinless chicken breasts	
4 tablespoons fruit chutney	
3 tablespoons chopped pecan nuts	
6 slices bacon	

1 **Combine the olive oil,** lime juice, coriander and salt and pepper. Using a sharp knife, cut a pocket in the thickest section of each chicken breast. Combine the chutney and nuts. Spoon 1 tablespoon of the chutney mixture into each breast pocket.

2 **Turn the tapered ends** of the chicken piece to the underside. Wrap a slice of bacon around each chicken breast to enclose the filling and secure with a toothpick.

3 **Put the chicken parcels** on a hot, lightly oiled barbecue grill or flat plate and cook for 5 minutes on each side, or until cooked through, turning once. Brush with the lime juice mixture several times during cooking and drizzle with any leftover lime juice mixture to serve.

Note: For a special touch, this recipe also works well with prosciutto, which is an Italian equivalent of bacon.

FIVE-SPICE ROAST CHICKEN

SERVES 4

1.8 kg (4 lb) chicken

1 tablespoon soy sauce

2 garlic cloves, crushed

1 teaspoon finely grated
   fresh ginger

1 tablespoon honey

1 tablespoon rice wine

1 teaspoon five-spice

1 tablespoon peanut oil

1 Wash the chicken and pat it thoroughly dry inside and out with paper towels. Whisk the soy sauce, garlic, ginger, honey, rice wine and five-spice together in a small bowl and brush it all over the chicken, ensuring every bit of skin is well coated. Put the chicken on a wire rack over a baking tray and refrigerate it, uncovered, for at least 8 hours, or overnight.

2 Preheat a kettle or covered barbecue to medium indirect heat and put a drip tray under the rack. Brush the chicken liberally with the peanut oil and put it breast-side up in the middle of the barbecue over the drip tray. Cover the barbecue and roast the chicken for 1 hour 10 minutes, or until the juices run clear when you pierce it with a skewer between the thigh and body. Check the chicken every so often, and if it appears to be over-browning, cover it loosely with foil. Leave it to rest, covered, for 10 minutes before carving and serving. The flavours in this style of chicken go particularly well with steamed Asian greens and fried rice.

HONEY MUSTARD CHICKEN

SERVES 4–6

175 g (6 oz/½ cup) honey

60 g (2¼ oz/¼ cup) dijon mustard

2 tablespoons oil

2 tablespoons white wine vinegar

3 garlic cloves, crushed

2 tablespoons chopped parsley leaves

1.8 kg (4 lb) chicken, cut into
10 serving pieces

1 Put the honey, mustard, oil, white wine vinegar, garlic, parsley and ¼ teaspoon freshly ground black pepper in a large, non-metallic bowl. Mix it all together well. Set aside 60 ml (2 fl oz/¼ cup) of the marinade to baste the chicken during cooking. Add the chicken pieces to the rest of the marinade and turn them so that they are thoroughly coated. Cover the bowl and refrigerate for at least 4 hours, or overnight.

2 Preheat a covered or kettle barbecue to medium indirect heat and cook the chicken pieces for 20–30 minutes, or until cooked through. The breast pieces may take as little as 15 minutes, while dark meat will take longer. Baste the chicken with the reserved marinade during the last 5–8 minutes of cooking, but no earlier or it is likely to burn. The chicken is delicious served on a bed of spring onion mash.

LEBANESE CHICKEN

250 g (9 oz/1 cup) plain Greek-style
  yoghurt

2 teaspoons soft brown sugar

4 garlic cloves, crushed

3 teaspoons ground cumin

1½ teaspoons ground coriander

1 small handful chopped flat-leaf
  (Italian) parsley

60 ml (2 fl oz/¼ cup) lemon juice

1 x 1.8 kg (4 lb) chicken, cut into
  10 serving pieces

cooking oil spray

1 Put the yoghurt, brown sugar, garlic, cumin, coriander, chopped parsley and lemon juice in a large non-metallic bowl and mix them together. Add the chicken pieces to the marinade and turn them so that they are completely coated, then cover and refrigerate for at least 2 hours, or overnight.

2 Lightly spray the barbecue plates with oil, then preheat the barbecue to medium direct heat. Take the chicken pieces out of the marinade and season them with salt and pepper. Cook the chicken pieces on the flat plate, turning them frequently, for 20–30 minutes, or until they are cooked through. If you have a barbecue with a lid, cover the barbecue while the chicken is cooking. This way, the breast pieces will take only 15 minutes to cook, while the pieces on the bone will take about 10 minutes longer. This dish is delicious served with eggplant and tomato salad sprinkled with sumac (a purplish lemon-flavoured spice).

MARGARITA CHICKEN

SERVES 4

4 chicken breasts, skin on, tenderloin and any excess fat removed

60 ml (2 fl oz/¼ cup) tequila

60 ml (2 fl oz/¼ cup) lime juice

2 small chillies, finely chopped

3 garlic cloves, crushed

1 large handful finely chopped coriander (cilantro) leaves

1 tablespoon olive oil

lime wedges

1 **Put the chicken,** tequila, lime juice, chilli, garlic, coriander and olive oil in a non-metallic bowl and mix it all together so that the chicken is coated in the marinade. Cover the bowl and refrigerate for at least 2 hours, or preferably overnight.

2 **Preheat a barbecue** chargrill to medium–high direct heat. Remove the chicken breasts from the marinade, season them with salt and pepper, and grill for 7–8 minutes on each side or until they are cooked through.

3 **Slice the chicken breasts** on the diagonal and serve with lime wedges. Delicious with avocado and grapefruit salad.

MIRIN AND SAKE CHICKEN

SERVES 4

4 large boneless, skinless chicken
  breasts

2 tablespoons mirin

2 tablespoons sake

1 tablespoon oil

5 cm (2 inch) piece of fresh ginger,
  very finely sliced

3 teaspoons soy sauce

salad leaves, to serve

1 **Put the chicken** in a non-metallic dish. Combine the mirin, sake and oil and pour over the chicken. Marinate for 15 minutes, then drain the chicken, reserving the marinade.

2 **Cook the chicken** on a hot, lightly oiled barbecue grill or flat plate for 4 minutes each side, or until tender.

3 **Put the ginger** in a pan and add the reserved marinade. Boil for about 7 minutes, or until thickened. Drizzle soy sauce over the chicken and top with the ginger. Serve immediately on a bed of salad leaves.

SAGE AND RICOTTA STUFFED CHICKEN

SERVES 4

250 g (9 oz/1 cup) fresh ricotta cheese, well drained

1 tablespoon shredded sage leaves

2 garlic cloves, crushed

1½ teaspoons grated lemon zest

40 g (1½ oz/⅓ cup) finely grated Parmesan cheese

4 boneless, skinless chicken breasts, tenderloin removed

8 thin slices prosciutto

olive oil, for brushing

1   **Combine ricotta, sage,** garlic, zest and parmesan until they are well mixed. Use a sharp knife to cut a large pocket into the side of each chicken breast and fill each pocket with a quarter of the ricotta mixture. Pin the pockets closed with toothpicks and wrap each breast in two slices of prosciutto, securing them with a toothpick.

2   **Heat a barbecue** flat plate to medium direct heat, brush the chicken parcels with olive oil and season them with freshly ground black pepper. Cook them for 8 minutes on each side, or until they are cooked through.

CRISPY CHICKEN WINGS

12 chicken wings

3 tablespoons soy sauce

3 tablespoons hoisin sauce

125 ml (4 fl oz/½ cup) tomato sauce

2 tablespoons honey

1 tablespoon soft brown sugar

1 tablespoon cider vinegar

2 garlic cloves, crushed

¼ teaspoon Chinese five-spice

2 teaspoons sesame oil

1 **Tuck chicken wing** tips to the underside and place in a non-metallic bowl. Mix together all the remaining ingredients and pour over the wings, tossing to coat. Cover and leave in the fridge for at least 2 hours, turning occasionally. Drain, reserving the marinade.

2 **Cook the wings** on a hot, lightly oiled barbecue grill or flat plate for 5 minutes, or until cooked through, brushing with the reserved marinade several times.

SPICY BUFFALO WINGS WITH RANCH DRESSING

SERVES 4

12 large chicken wings
2 teaspoons garlic salt
2 teaspoons onion powder
oil, for deep-frying
125 ml (4 fl oz/½ cup) tomato sauce
2 tablespoons worcestershire sauce

SAUCE
50 g (1¾ oz) butter, melted
Tabasco sauce, to taste

RANCH DRESSING
1 small garlic clove, crushed
185 g (¾ cup) mayonnaise
125 ml (4 fl oz/½ cup) buttermilk
2 tablespoons finely chopped flat-leaf (Italian) parsley
1 tablespoon finely chopped chives
1½ teaspoons lemon juice
1½ teaspoons dijon mustard
1 teaspoon onion powder

1 Pat the wings dry with paper towels, remove and discard the tip of each wing, then cut them in half at the joint. Combine the garlic salt, onion powder and 2 teaspoons of ground black pepper, and rub the spice mixture into each chicken piece.

2 Deep-fry chicken in batches for 2–3 minutes without letting it brown, then remove from the oil and drain on crumpled paper towels. When the chicken has cooled a little, put it in a non-metallic bowl with the combined tomato sauce, worcestershire sauce, butter and Tabasco, and toss so that all of the pieces are well coated in the marinade. Cover and refrigerate for at least 2 hours, or overnight.

3 To make the ranch dressing, mash the garlic and ¼ teaspoon salt to a paste, then add the mayonnaise, buttermilk, parsley, chives, lemon juice, mustard and onion powder and whisk it all together. Season well, cover and chill for at least 1 hour before serving.

4 Preheat a barbecue to medium direct heat. Cook the chicken for 6–8 minutes on each side, or until it is caramelised and sticky, turning and basting with the marinade as it cooks. Serve hot with the ranch dressing.

TARRAGON CHICKEN

SERVES 4

1½ tablespoons tarragon, chopped

1 garlic clove, crushed

50 g (1¾ oz) butter, softened

1.6 kg (3 lb 8 oz) whole chicken

2 teaspoons oil

150 ml (5 fl oz) chicken stock

1½ tablespoons white wine

1 tablespoon plain (all-purpose) flour

1 tablespoon tarragon leaves

150 ml (5 fl oz) thick (double/heavy) cream

1 **Preheat the oven** to 200°C (400°F/Gas 6). Combine the chopped tarragon, garlic and half the butter. Season with salt and pepper and place inside the cavity of the chicken. Tie the legs together and tuck the wing tips under.

2 **Heat the remaining butter** with the oil in a large flameproof casserole dish over low heat and brown the chicken on all sides. Add the chicken stock and wine. Cover the casserole and bake in the oven for 1 hour 20 minutes, or until the chicken is tender and the juices run clear when a thigh is pierced with a skewer. Remove the chicken, draining all the juices back into the casserole dish. Cover with foil and a tea towel (dish towel) and allow to rest.

3 **Skim a tablespoon** of the surface fat from the cooking liquid and put it in a small bowl. Skim the remainder of the fat from the surface and discard. Add the flour to the reserved fat and mix until smooth. Whisk quickly into the cooking liquid and stir over medium heat until the sauce boils and thickens.

4 **Strain the sauce** into a clean saucepan and add the tarragon leaves. Simmer for 2 minutes, then stir in the cream and reheat without boiling. Season with salt and pepper. Carve the chicken and spoon the sauce over the top to serve.

Note: This dish relies heavily on the quality of the bird; use an organic or corn-fed chicken for the best results, and be sure to use French tarragon for the best flavour.

CHICKEN WITH FORTY CLOVES OF GARLIC

SERVES 4

2 stalks celery, including leaves

2 sprigs rosemary, plus extra to garnish

4 sprigs thyme, plus extra to garnish

4 sprigs flat-leaf (Italian) parsley, plus extra to garnish

1.6 kg (3 lb 8 oz) whole chicken

40 cloves garlic, unpeeled

2 tablespoons olive oil

1 carrot, roughly chopped

1 small onion, cut into 4 wedges

250 ml (9 fl oz/1 cup) white wine

1 baguette, cut into slices

1   Preheat the oven to 200°C (400°F/Gas 6). Put a chopped celery stalk and 2 sprigs each of the rosemary, thyme and parsley into the chicken cavity. Add 6 garlic cloves. Tie the legs together and tuck the wing tips under.

2   Brush the chicken liberally with some of the oil and season well. Scatter about 10 more garlic cloves in a large saucepan. Put the remaining sprigs of herbs, chopped celery, carrot and onion in the saucepan.

3   Put the chicken into the saucepan. Scatter the remaining garlic cloves around the chicken and add the remaining oil and the wine. Cover and bake for 1 hour 20 minutes, or until the chicken is tender and the juices run clear when the thigh is pierced with a skewer.

4   To serve, carefully lift the chicken out of the saucepan. Drain the juices into a small saucepan. Remove the garlic cloves from the drained mixture and set aside. Spoon off the fat from the juices and boil for 2–3 minutes to reduce and thicken a little.

5   Cut the chicken into serving portions, pour over a little of the juices and scatter with the garlic. Toast the baguette slices, then spread with the soft flesh squeezed from the garlic. Garnish the chicken with herb sprigs and serve with the baguette slices.

Note: Serve the dish with buttered noodles or rice to soak up all the flavoursome juices.

INDEX